D1616889

OBJECT LOVE AND REALITY

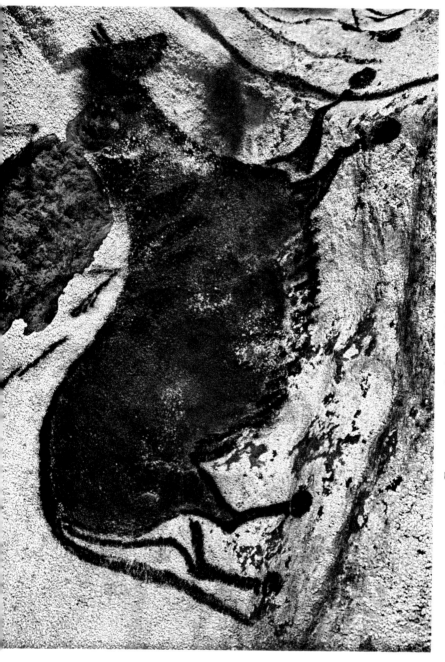

From a cave painting—Axial Gallery, Lascaux.

OBJECT LOVE AND REALITY

An Introduction to a Psychoanalytic
Theory of Object Relations

ARNOLD H. MODELL, M.D.

INTERNATIONAL UNIVERSITIES PRESS, INC.
NEW YORK

"The bird a nest, the spider a web, man friendship."

WILLIAM BLAKE

CONTENTS

ACKNOWLEDGMENTS

I am grateful to my friends and colleagues who have carefully read and criticized this manuscript and whose suggestions I have valued. I especially wish to thank Dr. David Beres and Mr. Irving Singer, Associate Professor of Philosophy at the Massachusetts Institute of Technology. I am also grateful to Dr. Ives Hendrick, who has been a source of constant encouragement, to Dr. Grete Bibring, Psychiatrist-in-Chief Emeritus of Beth Israel Hospital, and to my colleagues at that hospital, with whom I have been able to discuss and clarify many of the views presented here.

I also wish to thank the Psychiatric Service of Beth Israel Hospital and Dr. John Vorenberg, formerly Acting Psychiatrist-in-Chief, for their generous support which facilitated the preparation of the manuscript. Mrs. Penelope Wells, who typed earlier drafts and offered constant editorial criticism, and Mrs. Miriam Winkeller, who prepared the final version, have been invaluable to me.

I am indebted to Charles Scribner's Sons for permission to quote from Martin Buber's *I and Thou* and to the Yale University Press for permission to quote from Ernst Cassirer's *The Philosophy of Symbolic Forms*.

The frontispiece is taken from a cave painting. The original is at the Axial Gallery, Lascaux.

PREFACE

The theory of object relations, that is, love relationships taken in their broadest sense, refers to the realm of experience that is closest to the psychoanalyst's daily work. Yet psychoanalysis does not possess a satisfactory theory of object relations. The absence of such a theory can, in part, be attributed simply to the fact that Freud did not provide us with one. Freud's 1914 paper, "On Narcissism: An Introduction," had its observational roots in a phenomonology of schizophrenia that we now know to be one-sided and partly incorrect. The massive withdrawal of interest from loved objects and from the environment that Freud described does occur in some instances, but more commonly the schizophrenic maintains some form of object relation, albeit very primitive in nature. There is hardly any psychoanalyst today who would maintain, as Freud did, that the schizophrenic is incapable of forming a transference.

Although the psychoanalytic treatment of schizophrenia remains a highly specialized research activity, the treatment of the so-called borderline state has, with the widening scope of psychoanalysis, become quite common. Most psychoanalysts have treated such patients and there is an extensive literature describing the nature of the transference relationship. However, the absence of a unified theory of object relations has prevented psychoanalysts from sharing a common conceptual language, thus obscuring areas of fundamental clinical agreement. The lack of fit between theory and clinical experience has led some analysts, such as Fairbairn, to propose a radical revision of Freudian psychoanalytic theory. Although I am an admirer of Fairbairn's work, I cannot accept his theory, as he forces us to choose between Freud and Fairbairn, and what Fairbairn offers us does not compensate for the loss of Freud. Science is a conservative enterprise—it does not discard an old theory unless a new one is demonstrably better. Despite the limitation of Freud's (1914) paper, there is within Freud's works, as I hope to demonstrate, a latent theory of object relations that is more consonant with clinical experience.

The contributions of many contemporary analysts have, I believe, prepared the groundwork for a unified theory of object relations. Winnicott's description of the transitional object and the maternal "holding environment," Hartmann's theory of the ego's autonomous relation to the environment, Jacobson's and Erikson's studies of disorders of identity, and Hendrick's contribution to our understanding of early ego identifications have all made it possible for me to sketch here the outline of a unified psychoanalytic theory of object relations.

This book, then, represents an attempt at a synthesis, an attempt to bring Freud's theory of narcissism into better accord with more recent clinical knowledge of borderline and schizophrenic patients.

At the close of this work, I propose a schema that I hope will enable us to conceptualize progressive and regressive changes in object love. In constructing this schema, I have found it necessary to use both topographic and structural metaphors. Whether or not Freud intended structural theory to replace topographic theory, as has recently been suggested, I have found a topographic metaphor to be indispensable.

Chapter I

INTRODUCTION: PSYCHOANALYSIS AND OBJECT RELATIONS THEORY

The influence of theory upon observation in the development of science has been portrayed in a recent work by Kuhn (1962). What he has described for science in general has special relevance to psychoanalysis. According to Kuhn, it is a sense of progress that distinguishes science from other human enterprises with intellectual content, such as philosophy or religion. Progress in science does not consist of steady movement but is discontinuous. In fact, the impetus for much scientific work is the constant discrepancy between the facts of a science and its theory. The fit between theory and observation is always imperfect, but when it is good enough it promotes what Kuhn has described as "normal science," that is, the attempt to solve problems within the framework of an accepted theory. When the fit between theory and observation is known to be poor, the scientist experiences a great feeling of uncertainty and doubt, and he begins to wonder about the future of his science. This state of affairs is resolved by the formation of a new theory, one that affords a better fit, and the cycle is repeated. With each new conceptualization, older facts "are abandoned" if there is an absence of an appropriate conceptual language.

To a certain extent, the progress of Freud's thought corresponded to the pattern that Kuhn has suggested. Freud's

earliest theories (described as "topographic") were designed
to explain the phenomena that occupied his clinical attention, that is, repression and symptom formation. He formed
a model of the mind based primarily on the need to differentiate the quality of consciousness. As Freud's own experience
deepened and he became more aware of the stubbornness of
neurotic symptoms, a stubbornness that was determined in
part by an unconscious aspect of guilt, he was forced to consider that the quality of consciousness versus unconsciousness
was not the essential issue. Freud had previously believed that
what is unconscious and what is conscious was determined by
separate mental systems; he considered the forces of repression and the system of the unconscious to be antithetical. It
has been suggested (Gill, 1963; Arlow and Brenner, 1964)
that it was the recognition of the importance of unconscious
guilt that led Freud to a major revision of psychoanalytic
theory, a revision that has been described as "structural" theory. This revision acknowledged that the forces of repression
may themselves be unconscious. A new metaphor was introduced, the familiar tripartite image of ego, superego, and id.
The function of repression was attributed to the superego (a
differentiated portion of the ego), a function which remained,
at least in part, unconscious.

With the focus of theoretic attention upon ego psychology,
there was in the practice of psychoanalysis a corresponding
shift of interest away from the mechanism of symptom formation—analysis of character now became the principal aim of
psychoanalytic treatment. As is well known, there was a corresponding shift in technique, resulting in a lengthening of
psychoanalysis and a painstaking focus on the mechanisms of
unconscious ego defenses. (Anna Freud's, *The Ego and the
Mechanisms of Defense* [1936], belongs to this period of development.)

In this phase of psychoanalytic development, the relation
between theory and practice was one (in Kuhn's terminology)

of relatively good fit. It was a period of psychoanalysis marked by relative optimism—corresponding to what Kuhn has described as the workings of normal science.

Psychoanalysis has now entered a new period, where the relation between observation and theory results in a poorer fit. There has again been a shift in clinical experience which has been described as a "widening of the scope of psychoanalysis" (Stone, 1954). There has been a change in the nature of the patients who undergo psychoanalysis. To an increasing extent, psychoanalysts are now treating patients who might not have been considered suitable cases 20 or 30 years ago—patients who have been described variously as borderline psychotics, cases of ego distortion or impairment, or cases of severe narcissistic neuroses. The "classical hysteric" is now a rarity. There is, I believe, a fair uniformity of opinion amongst psychoanalysts who treat these patients regarding the bare facts of clinical observation; but there is a marked divergence of conceptual language. This cleavage between theory and observation is, I believe, growing and has contributed to a feeling of uncertainty regarding the value of particular aspects of psychoanalytic theory, an uncertainty that is not always openly acknowledged.

One immediate consequence of the absence of an acceptable theory is controversy concerning categories, that is to say, nosology. There is uncertainty as to whether these more disturbed people belong to the class of neurosis or psychosis. It has even been proposed that the concept of neurosis and psychosis be abandoned altogether (Menninger et al., 1963).[1]

---

[1] At this point I wish to make my own views clear. I have described this group of patients, from which my observations have been drawn, as borderline. For reasons which I hope will become more evident in later chapters, I consider this group to be psychotic rather than neurotic because of the quality of their transference love. In the transference relationship that is formed with these people there is a failure to distinguish inner from outer reality; there is, in brief, a failure of reality testing. This will be discussed in more detail in Chapters IV and VI.

Although I consider the borderline patient as one who demonstrates a pre-

This discrepancy between conceptual language and observation results from the lack of a satisfactory theory of object relations. Feelings of disquietude or uncertainty regarding the worth of psychoanalytic theory are most noticeable in those psychoanalysts whose clinical practice requires such a theory of object relations. I am referring to those psychoanalysts who treat seriously ill persons who have fundamental problems in adaptation to the external world and who have a fundamental disturbance in their capacity to form love relationships.

It is for this reason that many of the more recent attempts to revise or replace psychoanalytic theory have been made by those clinicians who have specialized in the treatment of borderline and psychotic patients. In this country, Harry Stack Sullivan's contributions have led to a strongly held point of view rather than a substitute for psychoanalytic theory, a view that underlines the importance of inadequate communication (in a one-to-one "interpersonal field") in the production of some forms of mental illness (Sullivan, 1953). In Britain, Fairbairn, a psychoanalyst who was especially experienced in the treatment of "schizoid" people, proposed a sweeping reformulation of psychoanalytic theory. A synopsis of his views was published in 1963, shortly before his death. Fairbairn's radical revision replaced Freud's instinct theory with the statement "Libido is a function of the ego and the ego is fundamentally object seeking." Fairbairn's

---

dominantly psychotic transference, I have differentiated this group from other forms of psychoses (Modell, 1963). As I shall describe (especially in Chapter VII), the distinguishing characteristics of this other group of patients, usually designated as schizophrenic, is their relationship to love objects. In contrast to *some* schizophrenics, the borderline patients' relationship to love objects and the external world is never abandoned. They evidence a great stability of character structure which permits them, in Gitelson's phrase, to "put themselves in the way of objects" (Gitelson, 1958).

I recognize that this definition of borderline is at variance with Knight's definition. Knight (1954) used the term "borderline" to refer to early or incipient schizophrenia.

theory was not intended to supplement Freud's theory but to supplant it. As an alternative to Freudian theory, Fairbairn's theory has won very few supporters, although many psychoanalysts, and I include myself in this group, have profited greatly from his understanding of the schizoid patient. And Melanie Klein, whose controversial theory proposes that object relations are established shortly after birth, has received the staunchest support from those analysts who have specialized in the treatment of psychosis (for example, Rosenfeld and Bion).

The inadequacy of a psychoanalytic theory of object relations may be partly due to Freud's limited experience with psychotic people, which led him to propose certain views that we now know to be inaccurate. In one instance, Freud was simply wrong when he described the schizophrenic person as one who was unable to form a transference. In another statement, which has had even greater significance for a psychoanalytic theory of object relations, Freud was, I believe, not incorrect but incomplete in his views. Freud asserted that the *fundamental* process in schizophrenia was the withdrawal of libidinal interest from loved objects and from the external world. Such a massive withdrawal from love objects in schizophrenia does occur in *some* patients at certain times in the course of their illness. There are other psychotic people who possess a certain stability of character similar to that which I have described for borderline cases (Modell, 1963), so that in these cases the withdrawal that Freud describes as fundamental does not occur. These people maintain relationships with love objects and yet in terms of their disturbance of reality testing must be considered psychotic.[2]

The psychopathology of schizophrenia and its related dis-

[2] The fact that object relations are maintained by some schizophrenics has led Arlow and Brenner (1964) to assert that the massive withdrawal that Freud described does not occur at all. I cannot agree with this statement. (For further discussion of this point see Chapters VI and VII).

orders is not only of interest to the specialist. Freud believed that the study of psychosis would afford us the deepest insight into the early development of the mind; the knowledge obtained from the study of schizophrenia led to Freud's paper *On Narcissism* (1914). If clinical experience forces new observations upon us, the theory of narcissism itself must be reconsidered.

Psychoanalytic investigation of the borderline and psychotic individual has led to the development of concepts such as the "disorder of identity,"[3] concepts which have yet to be fully articulated with more basic psychoanalytic theory, as the concept of identity was not described by Freud. It is not a "basic psychoanalytic concept." Glover, a defender of "classical psychoanalytic theory," offers the following acerbic response to Jacobson's monograph (Glover, 1966):

> As for the terms 'identity diffusion' and 'identity disorder,' the least said the soonest mended in my opinion. Either they mean little or nothing or they comprise the whole of psychoanalytic psychology. . . .

It is understandable then that men like Fairbairn, when faced with these problems, would wish to rip out the entire fabric of psychoanalytic thinking and start anew. A rival theory, in order to be viable, must be able to compete successfully with its predecessor, and Fairbairn's theory has not, in my opinion, survived this competition. It would take a man of Freud's genius to rival Freud, and the history of science shows that such men do not appear in every generation; they scarcely appear in every century. So we must attempt to do collectively what Freud did singlehanded, to modify theory in accordance with observation.

---

[3] See Jacobson for a discussion of the concept of identity that has developed from the treatment of borderline cases and her critical examination of Erikson's concept of identity (Jacobson, 1964).

I believe that the lines of direction of necessary alteration of psychoanalytic theory are discernible within Freud's works. There is in Freud, I submit, a latent but not a manifest theory of object relations.

I must try, however, at this point to correct a certain impression that the reader may have received from my earlier description of orderly stages in the development of Freud's thinking. Those who wish to present Freud's work as a systematic theory—that is, a body of highly articulated hypotheses that form "laws" of the psychic apparatus, laws analogous to those of the precise sciences—are imposing an organization that does not exist in Freud's work itself. With the possible exception of *The Interpretation of Dreams* (1900), Freud's major contributions—the papers *On Narcissism* (1914), *The Ego and the Id* (1923), *Group Psychology* (1921), and *Inhibitions, Symptoms and Anxiety* (1926)—are not finished contributions. Freud's mind was intensely disciplined, but it was not as neat and orderly as the "systematizers" of psychoanalysis would have us believe. Within a given paper, Freud presented established clinical observations as well as impressions that are but dimly apprehended, impressions which provide suggestions for future investigation. That is why it is possible to discern in Freud's earliest work the outlines of a future ego psychology. The transition from what has been termed "topographic theory" to what is now "structural theory" may not represent a sharply demarcated change in Freud's thinking. Elements of structural concepts were present in Freud's thinking from the beginning—elements that foreshadowed the direction in which psychoanalytic theory would move. For this reason I believe that we can find a similar outline for a psychoanalytic theory of object relations, an outline that is already discernible in Freud's later works.

If we place the theory of object relations within the broader context of the ego's relation to the external world, I believe that we will discover this latent outline. The reader may immediately object that human love relations and the external world are not synonymous. From the standpoint of rational thought this is of course true, but if we consider the early development of the mind, we know that for the young child the mother and the environment are indeed synonymous.[4] And it has been known since 1913, with the publication of Ferenczi's important paper, "Stages in the Development of the Sense of Reality" (Ferenczi, 1913), that the growth of object love and the acceptance of the pain of the external world is an inseparable process.

The editors of Freud's *Standard Edition* (Vol. XIX, p. 143) note that from 1923 onwards Freud's attention shifted from an interest in the mechanism of repression to an examination of the problem of denial (which has been translated as "disavowal"). In contrast to repression, which defends against the dangers arising from within, that is, from the instincts, denial is directed against the pain of the external world—which is implicitly the pain that ensues from object loss (to which, in the male, the idea of castration is added). This line of thought was developed by Freud in the series of papers, *The Loss of Reality in Neurosis and Psychosis* (1924a); *Fetishism* (1927); and the unfinished posthumous paper, *Splitting of the Ego in the Process of Defence* (1940b). Freud makes the most direct acknowledgment of the role of object loss in the development of the capacity to test reality in his very important paper on *Negation* (1925).

It is the purpose of this monograph to attempt to synthesize the newer knowledge gained from the observation of transference love in psychotic patients, with these ideas that Freud was beginning to develop. This will, of necessity, en-

---

[4] Searles (1960) has maintained that there is a basic relatedness to the nonhuman environment that exists even in regressed schizophrenics. However, he has not, in my opinion, demonstrated that the individual in such regressed states is able to differentiate an animate from an inanimate environment. I would argue that such a nonanimistic view of the world is a later acquisition in the development of both the individual and the culture (see Chapter II).

tail a modification of Freud's earlier concept of narcissism. These theoretical issues will be discussed especially in the final two chapters—Chapters VIII and IX. The term "narcissism" as a descriptive adjective is indispensable; it has become part of our everyday language. However, as a basic concept it is, as I hope to show, too complex and covers too many different kinds of phenomena to be fully serviceable.[5] Basic concepts should possess a unifying simplicity.

What I shall present to the reader in the following chapters will not consist of new observations concerning borderline or psychotic people, for my own clinical experience is very much in accord with what Jacobson and Winnicott have already described; I shall instead present these observations from a somewhat different focus. It is my hope that this change of focus may lead to a psychoanalytic theory of object relations.

---

[5] For example, narcissism describes both the state where the ego is invested with libido following object loss, such as schizophrenic megalomania, and earlier stages of object love which are also termed "narcissistic." Waelder (1960) has made a similar point, noting that the term "narcissism" is used to describe the condition of both the person who seems not to need anyone else and the person who is in great need of constant support.

Chapter II

MAGIC, OMNIPOTENCE, AND ANXIETY

The relation between prehistoric modes of thought and psychoanalytic theory may seem obscure. There is, however, an analogy between the historical development of society's gradual acceptance of an inanimate, unmoved world, and the developmental process in the individual that permits the acceptance of "reality." For in *Totem and Taboo* (1913) Freud showed magical thinking to be common to both the *inner world* of modern man and the *social institutions* of prehistoric man. Freud suggested that magical thinking served analogous functions in neurotic symptoms and primitive social institutions. We intend to demonstrate in this chapter that magical thinking is not only a formal category of thought, but that it is a basic mode of the ego's relationship to the human and inanimate environment.

The distinctions between the observer and the observed, between subject and object, between the mental and the physical—distinctions that form our basic assumptions concerning the environment—were alien to prehistoric man (Frankfort et al., 1949, and Cassirer, 1953). The concepts of an unmoved, inanimate nature are not innate assumptions but are themselves the product of civilization; the concept of "reality" and the concept of "an environment" are not "givens" but are themselves the result of a considerable cultural achievement.

The earliest period of man's intellectual history has been referred to as the period of animism. It would be more accurate to use the term "preanimism," for strictly speaking, primitive man does not distinguish between the animate and the inanimate. This does not mean that primitive man, in order to explain natural phenomena, imparts human characteristics to an inanimate world—primitive man simply does not know an inanimate world (Frankfort et al., 1949).

The Meaning and Function of Paleolithic Art

Knowledge of primitive societies has been derived from archeological records and from ethnology, the study of contemporary primitives. Rapidly vanishing contemporary stone-age societies, such as the Australian aborigines, are themselves very ancient. Therefore, their cultural institutions, although primitive, have a long and probably complex history.[1] Furthermore, these people are not our direct ancestors but are cultural offshoots who, for some as yet unknown reason, remain arrested in their cultural growth.[2]

While we have no direct access to the mind of our most ancient ancestors, we can attempt a reconstruction of the early stages of our own society from the record of stone-age art which has been, by chance, preserved for us. The chance survival in caves of the artistic products of Cro-Magnon man provides some insight into the mind of our most remote ancestors. The significance of these discoveries has not yet been

[1] This is shown, for example, in the variegated forms of totemism as a social institution that is practiced by the Australian aborigines (Lévi-Strauss, 1963.)

[2] There is suggestive evidence that the Australian aborigines deteriorated from a higher to a lower culture. The wild dog of Australia, the dingo, is believed by Lorenz to be a formerly domesticated animal that arrived with the original settlers. When the level of culture of the original inhabitants deteriorated, the dog reverted to its former undomesticated state (Lorenz, 1954).

sufficiently appreciated by anthropology and psychology (Read, 1965).

Paleolithic cave art was known in the nineteenth century, but the authorities then could not believe that work of such skill, subtlety, and beauty could be produced by prehistoric man. Such examples as did exist were generally dismissed by the learned community as either outright frauds or artifacts of comparatively recent origin. It was not until the twentieth century that the great antiquity of cave art was accepted. Modern methods of dating, by means of radioactive carbon, indicate that Paleolithic relics at two sites are between 15,000 and 24,000 years old (Graziosi, 1960).

The upper Paleolithic era is associated with the last expansion of the Wurm glaciation. The age of cave art corresponds with the appearance in Europe of Homo sapiens (Cro-Magnon), who was destined to replace Neanderthal man. There is irrefutable evidence that the art that we shall describe was produced by Homo sapiens and not Neanderthal man. The Neanderthal people did practice a ritual burial. The dead were placed in certain specified positions and fine weapons were frequently buried alongside males. However, cave art was not part of their culture. Paleolithic art then is evidence of a quantum jump of mental capacity, of an intellectual mutation that separated Homo sapiens from his predecessors; a quantum jump of mind that established the adaptive superiority of Homo sapiens which eventually led to the extinction of the less intelligent Neanderthals.

The great skill of these artists suggests that the art itself may have had a prehistory, a gradual emergence from earlier, cruder forms that are now lost to us. However, no evidence of earlier forms has yet been discovered.[3] It is thought that these Cro-Magnon people migrated to Europe from the East. Therefore, it is possible that the prehistory of Paleolithic art

[3] Leroi-Gourhan (1966) describes the development of this art from crude to more sophisticated forms. However, his assertions remain controversial.

may be discovered along the migratory route. But this remains a conjecture.

At present Paleolithic cave art has been discovered in nearly a hundred separate sites in Southern Europe, concentrated for the most part in Northern Spain and Southwestern France, with some scattered finds in Italy and Sicily (Graziosi, 1960). Important discoveries continue to be made so that we have reasonable expectations that our knowledge will continue to grow; the best known and finest examples of Paleolithic art, in the cave of Lascaux, were not unearthed until 1940.

The appearance of this art at a given point in time, its practice extending over possibly ten centuries, followed by its extinction, suggests that a true intellectual revolution had taken place, analogous to the revolution that occurred in Greece about 14,000 years later—a renaissance followed again by dark ages. Although individual differences exist from site to site, there is remarkable homogeneity to the art, suggesting that the art itself is the expression of a social institution. The paintings are also associated in time with artifacts sculptured in stone and animal horn. The most significant example of this so-called mobiliary art is a small statue of a female. The uniform style of execution of these figures found over a wide area of Europe supports the conjecture that they are an object of worship. They have been called "Venuses"—in that they are invariably carved with exaggerated breasts, genitals, and buttocks. This exaggeration of the generative organs of the female body strongly suggests the worship of a mother goddess—the source of life. G. Rachel Levy (1963) has traced the cultural inheritance of elements of this Stone Age religion and has shown that elements of this early religion became incorporated into Greek culture and hence became a permanent part of Western civilization.

There have been numerous explanations of the function of this Paleolithic art. Some consider it to be merely an ex-

pression of "art for art's sake," an example of playful surplus
energy, a joyous decoration. One author, for example, inter-
prets cave art as an illustration of Huizinga's homo ludens
(Bataille, 1955). This view has been almost entirely replaced
with what is for us a much more convincing assertion—this
is not decorative art; this art served a magico-religious function that was *essential* to life.

Although man still lives in a world of unpredictable dangers—he may be killed by disease or by an automobile, and
there is the everpresent threat of atomic destruction—these
dangers are not immediately present to the senses and can
thus be considered relatively remote. It takes an effort of the
imagination to reconstruct the frightful proximity of death
faced by early man (Murray, 1951). The creators of these
paintings lived in an inhospitable climate; Southern Europe
was much colder then than it is today; they had only flint
weapons with which to defend themselves against dangerous
animals such as cave lions and the woolly rhinoceros. But
most important, the difference between survival and prolifer-
ation and death and extinction was the success of the hunt.
These people were exclusively hunters. Game was captured
by means of flint-tipped spears and arrows and traps, or it
was driven over the sides of cliffs.

If cave art was meant to serve a decorative purpose we
would expect the art to be easily accessible and associated
with caves that were used as family dwellings. Observation
gives no support to this theory. We are led to the unmis-
takable conclusion that the cave art served a religious function arising from this primitive society's proximity to death
(Rochlin, 1965).

The paintings are found for the most part in deep, dark
recesses of limestone caves. They were made by the light of
oil lamps, fragments of which have been discovered at the
sites (Childe, 1951). Many of the paintings (Lascaux, for example) appear on the ceilings of the caves and must have

presented an extraordinarily difficult task of execution. As we have mentioned earlier, the homogeneity of style, extending over wide geographic areas, and the associated mother-goddess figures, suggest that these cave shrines are the tangible remains of an archaic religion. These caves were holy shrines, sacred places for the performance of magical rites. The paintings are almost entirely of animals, portrayed in a style that is subtle, vital, and naturalistic (Read, 1965). The animals, in characteristic poses, appear to be captured in motion and are portrayed with such skill and accuracy that modern zoologists can correctly identify species that are now extinct (Laming, 1959). The world at that time contained at least as many animal species as are living today if not more. Yet relatively few groups of animals are chosen for representation: horses, oxen, reindeer, bison, lions, bears, and rhinoceroses. The animals form two groups: those needed for food, and those that are most dangerous. Hyenas, wolves, reptiles, fishes, and birds were seldom portrayed (Laming, 1959). Many of the paintings are superimposed over each other, the artist repeatedly using the same space although other spaces on the cave walls were available. This suggests that a specific site was sacred and that the multiple images may relate to the practice of reproductive magic (Breuil and Obermaier, 1935). When two animals compose a scene, they are invariably male and female, again suggesting reproductive magic (Graziosi, 1960). At some sites animals are actually portrayed in the act of copulation—a celebrated clay statue was found consisting of bisons in the act of copulation (Graziosi, 1960). In addition, mares are frequently portrayed as pregnant.

There is a famous engraving in the cave at Les Trois Freres called The Sorcerer. It is a finely engraved figure of a man with exposed human genitals. The head is shown with two large stag antlers. The figure has a large tail which might be that of a horse. It is shown in the act of dancing, with the body flexed forward and legs bent in movement (Graziosi,

1960). Traces of paint adhere to the forehead and nose, suggesting the representation of a man wearing an animal mask or possibly the representation of a god. In front of this "sorcerer" are tangled, superimposed drawings of animals, a veritable Noah's Ark, all portrayed with exquisite accuracy. This scene, in conjunction with the other evidences of reproductive magic, suggests a belief that this sorcerer or "god" is *literally* creating the animal species. This may be evidence of the first myth of creation, a myth of hitherto unimaginable antiquity.

In other scenes countless bisons, horses, reindeer, etc., are engraved or painted with weapons transfixing their bodies (Graziosi, 1960). In Niaux, arrows are engraved within an outline of a bison, next to cavities produced by the dripping of water upon the stone. The cavities are interpreted as representation of the animal's wounds. The Paleolithic artist tended to make use of the actual characteristics of the surface of the cave walls; the created environment and the "real" environment, that is, the solid earth, were interpenetrated. We shall return later to discuss the significance of this observation.

Many of the animals are placed near abstract, geometric designs that have been interpreted as the symbolic representation of animal traps. There is a figure of a horse engraved in clay in the cave at Montespan, which is pockmarked with holes produced by spear thrusts, so that it is likely that many of the painted sacred grottos were the scene of ritualistic dances.

In the cave paintings life is both created and destroyed. Cave art functions as a creative illusion, an illusion that provides for the participant a sense, through symbolic representation, of mastery, a mastery of the elemental forces of life and death. Action upon the symbolic animal influenced the "real" animal, creating a world that acknowledged no distinction between symbol and object, a world that was created in accordance with omnipotent wishes.[4] For this hunting community, assuring the supply and destruction of game was the assurance of life itself. We can trace analogous practices many centuries later, when man learned to raise crops. In Neolithic agricultural society the fertility of the crops determined whether man would survive or perish, so that the magical practices of that age were directed toward a changing need. In areas dependent upon rainfall, religious beliefs focused skyward on the making of rain; in other areas dependent upon irrigation, magical practices assured the continuity of cyclic phenomena, such as the rising and setting of the sun. I do not wish to trace this story any further. I only wish to demonstrate that although the dangers from the environment may change, the magical methods of dealing with the sense of helplessness remain the same.

The basic needs of all hunting societies are similar: to kill the game needed for food, to destroy dangerous species, and to ensure the rebirth of that which is destroyed—to assure the continuity of life. As Freud has shown in *Totem and Taboo* the primitive man's relationship to the environment is basically ambivalent; the environment provides the cycle of death and creation. Reparation must be made for that which is destroyed. Frazer mentions the devices by which "the savage seeks to atone for the wrong done by him to his animal vic-

4 We do not intend to suggest that this exhausts the possible interpretations of cave art, for our evidence is much too fragmentary to suggest that. Some recent studies suggest additional meanings. Leroi-Gourhan (1966) proposes that the pairing of animal species and the placement of these species in specified parts of the cave have symbolic meaning. He believes that horses symbolize masculinity and bisons femininity. Also, he is of the opinion that the paintings are used for more elaborate and sophisticated symbolization, as compared to the explanation (which we have followed) that the paintings support a sympathetic hunting magic. While Leroi-Gourhan's interpretation is controversial, even if he is correct in his belief that sexual elements are symbolized, one may still conclude that the symbolic creation is intended to influence the real world. A possible interpretation could be that the juxtaposition of male and female elements is intended to assure the continued generation of life.

tims." Frazer noted that the primitive worship of animals assumes two forms: on one hand, animals are worshipped and therefore, neither killed nor eaten, whilst on the other hand, animals are worshipped because they are killed and eaten (Frazer, 1890, p. 479). A taboo placed upon the totem animal, therefore, does not preclude the eating of the sacred animal; however, reparation must be made. The specific forms of the Paleolithic religion (that is, the extent to which it is related to totemistic beliefs) is not our prime concern. As Freud noted earlier, what is institutionalized, what was public in primitive society, survives in the *inner world* of man in modern society; what once was public has now become private. We have examined these tangible products of this early culture in order to form some estimate of the quality of mind, that is, the magical or mythical modes of thought, of early man.

Cassirer's Concept of Mythical Thought

Magical thought is usually classified in accordance with Frazer's distinction between sympathetic and contagious magic (Frazer, 1890).

> First, that like produces like, effect resembling cause; second, that things which have once been in contact continue ever after to act on each other. The former principle may be called the law of similarity; the latter that of contact or contagion. Practices based on the law of similarity may be termed homeopathic magic; those based on the law of contact or contagion, contagious magic [p. 7].

As a descriptive account, Frazer's classification has served us well. However, Cassirer's monumental study of the formal aspects of mythical thinking has provided us with a more unifying schema that supplants Frazer's distinction between sympathetic and contagious magic. What is essential for magical thought is that the symbol used to represent the environ-mental object does not *denote* the object, but *is* the object; symbol and object are inextricably fused—they represent an inseparable unity. The form of the symbol may be, as in Paleolithic art, an image, or the symbol may be mimed, as in a ritual dance. The painting of the Paleolithic hunter does not represent a horse, it *is* a horse (Cassirer, 1953).

But if we examine myth itself, what it is and what it knows itself to be, we see that the separation of the ideal from the real, the distinction between the world of immediate reality and a world of mediate signification, this opposition of "image" and "object," is alien to it. Only observers who no longer live in it but reflect on it read such distinctions into myth. Where we see mere "representation," myth, insofar as it is not yet derived from its fundamental and original form, sees real identity. The "image" does not represent the "thing"; it *is* the thing; it does not merely stand for the object, but has the same actuality, so that it replaces the thing's immediate presence [p. 38].

Cassirer (1953) states further:

Yet this is no mere process of reflection, no product of pure meditation. It is not mere meditation but action which constitutes the center from which man undertakes the spiritual organization of reality. It is here that a separation begins to take place between the spheres of the objective and subjective, between the world of the I and the world of things. . . . Accordingly the world of mythical ideas, precisely in its first and most immediate forms, appears closely bound up with the world of efficacy. Here lies the core of the magical world view, which is saturated with this atmosphere of efficacy, which is indeed nothing more than a translation and transposition of the world of subjective emotions and drives into a sensuous, objective existence. The first energy by which man places himself as an independent being in opposition to things is that of desire. In desire he no longer simply accepts the world and the reality of things, but builds them up for himself. This is man's first and most primitive consciousness of his ability to give form to reality [p. 157].

The nature of mythical thought is essentially a psychological problem. As Freud (1913) stated in *Totem and Taboo,* "we are thus prepared to find that primitive man transposed the structural conditions of his own mind into the external world" (p. 91).

Child Development and the Concept of Omnipotence

The magical relation to the environment is dominated by the wish. The apparent separateness of objects in space is disavowed by the creative illusion of magical thoughts. Frazer's concept of contagious magic, that parts of the object are inseparable, and Cassirer's observation that the symbol and the object are inseparable, assert a belief in action at a distance. That is, despite the apparent physical separation of objects, there exists a connectedness between the symbol and the environmental object that is symbolized. The religious paintings of the Paleolithic period can be interpreted as symbols of objects that they denote, but there is little doubt that for Cro-Magnon man they were not symbols: the paintings and statues *were* the animals, and action upon the image would affect the object. The wishes expressed by means of magical thinking are determined by "real" needs and are the direct response to "real" dangers of the environment. There is a striking parallel between the response to a situation of helplessness, or, as we shall now say, anxiety, of Paleolithic man and the response to a situation of helplessness in the modern infant and child. Both create an environment where the spatial separation of subject and object is denied, where action takes place at a distance, and where action upon a symbol can affect the object.

Freud (1926), in *Inhibitions, Symptoms and Anxiety,* observed that man (as compared with other animals) is sent into the world "in a less finished state" (p. 154). So that the dangers of the external world are of greater importance. Freud further suggested that in this immature state man was less protected than are other animals by their considerable repertoire of innate, stereotyped reactions to danger; instead, man places his reliance on the protection of an external object:

> Small children are constantly doing things which endanger their lives, and that is precisely why they cannot afford to be without a protecting object. In relation to the traumatic situation in which the subject is helpless, external and internal dangers, real dangers and instinctual demands converge [Freud, 1926, p. 168].

During World War II Freud's daughter, Anna, substantiated her father's statements by observing children's reactions to the bombing of London (A. Freud and Burlingham, 1944). They observed that, contrary to expectation, very young children were not traumatized even if they were exposed to repeated bombings, provided that they were not separated from their mothers or mother substitutes. The situation was vastly different if the children were separated from the protective object. Furthermore, these authors observed that young children will share their mother's anxiety —that is, if the mother remains calm in the face of bombings, so will the child. Because of the child's primitive animal tie to its mother, the younger the child, the more the anxiety of the mother will impart itself upon the child. For the young child the environment is narrowed down to the mother—we might say that the environment *is* the mother. The possibility of loss of the maternal object is signaled by separation anxiety. Freud considered that each developmental phase has its own particular source of anxiety and that separation anxiety is characteristic of the earliest stage of development. This is followed in later periods by castration anxiety and what Freud referred to as superego anxiety. In the adult mind the content of anxiety referable to these different stages of development becomes condensed. Loss of an object is not fully distinguished from loss of the penis, and a superego anxiety may be manifested as a fear of death (Freud, 1926):

> I am therefore inclined to adhere to the view that the fear of death should be regarded as analogous to the fear of castration and that the situation to which the ego was reacting is one of being abandoned by the protecting superego—the powers of destiny—so that it has no longer any safeguard against all the dangers that surround it [p. 130].[5]

The child's relationship to his first object, as primitive man's relationship to a totemic animal, is fundamentally ambivalent. The object that is eaten is "all gone": it needs to be re-created. Freud observed that anxiety results not only from the actual separation from parental objects but that helplessness would result from a "growing tension due to need" (p. 137). That is to say that instinctual demands made upon parental objects, to the extent that these demands will threaten the relationship with the parental objects, implicitly threatens the loss of the object. Therefore the danger of separation is not limited to the danger of actual, physical separation from the protecting parental object, but may also arise as a result of the fundamental ambivalent instinctual wishes that the child experiences toward the parents. Freud believed that the child's ego permitted the development of certain mental processes that serve to forestall the experience of helplessness and catastrophic anxiety. If anxiety can be

[5] Freud considered that in the female, castration is not feared as it is already believed to have taken place. Hence, the girl fears not so much loss of an imagined phallus but loss of love.

experienced in small doses, it could serve as a "rescuing signal." *We suggest that the capacity for magical thought mitigates the danger of catastrophic anxiety through the creation of an illusion of lack of separateness between the self and the object.*

The parallel development that we have been referring to in primitive man and the modern child is as follows: Signal anxiety is the motive for defense. It is the motive of the institution of a magical, created environment that serves to mitigate the danger of the experience of total helplessness. So that the motives for the development of culture and the motives for the development of the inner life of the child converge and find a common meeting ground. The young child's inner world is one that is dominated by wishes and corresponds in the formal sense to the model of mythical thought that Cassirer outlines. That is, that symbols are not used in a denotive sense but *"are"* the objects denoted. In the psychoanalysis of adults, when one reaches the earliest possible levels, one discovers a similar mode of thought, a magical mode, or, as we shall now say, an omnipotent mode. The term "omnipotence of thought" was introduced by Freud (1913) in *Totem and Taboo* where he states:

> By way of summary, then, it may be said that the principle governing magic, the technique of the animistic mode of thinking, is the principle of the 'omnipotence of thought.'

For Freud then the concepts of magic and omnipotence were equivalent.[6]

Omnipotence or magical belief is in a sense a compensation

6 We fully accept Freud's equation of the omnipotent and the magical. However, for students of the history of religion, this terminology may be somewhat confusing, for certain historians of religion tend to distinguish the concept of omnipotence from the concept of magical thought which precedes it (Weber, 1922). To attribute the powers of omnipotence to a god was thought to be evidence of a belief in a transcendental being, a more advanced belief as compared to primitive magic and animism.

for the fact of prolonged biological helplessness of the human infant. In accordance with the human infant's fundamentally ambivalent relationship to his environment, that is, his mother, the structure of magical thought is also ambivalent. The need to create and the need to kill, the cycle of birth and destruction, of love and atonement, finds its expression in the child's belief in an omnipotent force of limitless goodness and unlimited destruction. The ambivalent nature of omnipotence finds its parallels in the concepts of manna and taboo in the primitive, of the experience of ecstasy, of union with the unlimited good, in contrast to the fear of destructive demons. The self or the environment may be experienced by the child as possessing omnipotent attributes (Jacobson, 1964). This phase of mental life is dominated by processes that have been termed introjection and projection, so that there is a constant oscillation—experiencing the attributes of omnipotence now in the self and now in the environment. This mode of thought, in a certain sense, gives form and structure to the child's first environment, that is, to the mother. In a certain sense, as we have seen earlier, from the work of Anna Freud and Burlingham, the mother *is* the environment.

Some child analysts have suggested that if the mother is able to provide the breast (or bottle) when the child desires it, this happy feeding relationship may reinforce the child's belief in his own omnipotence (Winnicott, 1951). That is to say, if the breast comes when he wishes it, he may develop a sense that there is something powerful and good inside of him. This sense of positive omnipotence, possessing something in oneself that is good, may be a necessary precondition for creativity in the adult. Conversely, the absence of intuitive mothering may strengthen the negative omnipotence leading to the belief that one possesses unlimited powers for destruction, as is seen in borderline and schizophrenic illness where love objects are believed to be endangered by one's omnipotent destructiveness. Omnipotent beliefs are, therefore, universal—they form the earliest core of the self-image. The quality of early maternal care may strengthen the positive or the negative side of omnipotent belief. An intuitive, "good" mother who presents the breast or bottle when it is desired may strengthen the child's belief in positive omnipotence; conversely, a frustrating mother may strengthen the negative side.

An Infant's Game

No matter how skillful or intuitive, the mother of a young child or infant cannot expect to meet the child's needs all of the time. Children's wishes know no limitations. Such conflicts with the environment that give rise to anxiety and the danger of catastrophic helplessness are avoided (in part) by means of magical thinking. Freud (1920) provided an excellent example in the following observation of a one-and-a-half-year-old child, who was later identified as his own grandchild.

I have been able, through a chance opportunity which presented itself, to throw some light on the first game played by a little boy of one and a half and invented by himself. It was more than a fleeting observation, for I lived under the same roof as the child and his parents for some weeks, and it was some time before I discovered the meaning of the puzzling activity which he constantly repeated.

The child was not at all precocious in his intellectual development. At the age of one and a half he could say only a few comprehensible words; he could also make use of a number of sounds which expressed a meaning intelligible to those around him. He was, however, on good terms with his parents and their one servant girl, and tributes were paid to his being a 'good boy.' He did not disturb his parents at night, he conscientiously obeyed orders not to touch certain things or go into certain rooms, and above all he never cried when his mother left him for a few hours. At the time, he was greatly attached to his mother, who not only fed him herself but had also looked after him without any outside help. This good little boy, however, had an occasional disturbing habit of taking any small objects he can get hold of and throwing them away from him into a corner, under the bed, and so on, so that hunting for his toys and picking them up was often quite a business. As he did this he gave vent to a loud, long drawn-out 'O-o-o-o' accompanied by an expression of interest and satisfaction. His mother and the writer of the present account were agreed in thinking that this was not a mere interjection but represented the German word 'fort' (gone). I eventually realized that it was a game and that the only use he made of any of his toys was to play "gone" with them. One day I made an observation which confirmed my view. The child had a wooden reel with a piece of string tied around it. It never occurred to him to pull it along the floor behind him, for instance, and play at its being a carriage. What he did was to hold the reel by the string and very skillfully throw it over the edge of his curtained cot, so that it disappeared into it, at the same time uttering his expressive, 'O-o-o-o.' He then pulled the reel out of the cot again by the string and hailed its reappearance with a joyful 'Da' (there). This, then, was the complete game—disappearance and return. As a rule one only witnesses its first act, which was repeated untiringly as a game in itself, though there was no doubt that the greater pleasure was attached to the second act [p. 14].

Freud interpreted the game as a reenactment of the painful departure of his mother which was accepted in reality (that is, an instinctual renunciation had been made). Through magical gesture the child created an illusion that he could control his mother's going and coming. The ritualized, mimetic actions of the game can be understood as symbolic processes of the child's inner world. The inner world, in this sense, replicates conflicts that the ego experiences in relationship to the environment, and, by removing the conflict from the external world, provides an illusion of mastery. The symbolic re-creation in the inner world of an event in the external world involves a reversal of roles (it is a symbolic microcosm of the outer world created in accordance with need).

The elements of the child's game are in a formal sense no different from the basic formula presented by mythical thought. The symbol *is* the object denoted; action upon the symbol can affect the object—a belief in action at a distance and a belief that serves the function of negating the perception of the physical separation of objects—the fact that objects can be lost.

Chapter III

THE TRANSITIONAL OBJECT: THE CREATED ENVIRONMENT

The Autonomous Relationship to the Environment

Before proceeding further I wish to correct a possible source of misunderstanding. In my description of preanimism and the environment that is structured by the child's omnipotent wish, I have neglected to describe another relationship to the environment that exists side by side with this more plastic process. This other relationship is more rigidly determined by certain structures that are innate, that is, the result of an evolutionary process.

Hartmann is responsible for the introduction of this concept into psychoanalytic theory, and his contribution remains one of the most important emendations of Freud's concept of the reality principle (Hartmann, 1939). Freud assumed that the "ego owes its origin as well as most of its acquired characteristics to its relation to the external world" (Freud, 1940a, p. 201). Freud did not dismiss the possibility that some portions of the ego might be innate but did not fully appreciate its implication with regard to the concept of the reality principle. Hartmann's view, which has subsequently been substantiated by observation of early infantile development (Spitz, 1965), is that the ego contains certain prestructured, biologically given modes of adaptation to the environment. It is not created entirely anew as a result of conflict, as Freud had supposed. Hartmann saw the need for two reality principles—one a prefigured, innate mode of adaptation (we can now say a genetic code of instruction) the other the result of conflict and idiosyncratic experience. Hartmann (1939) states:

> We may have before us a relationship to the external world which, as an independent factor, regulates certain prerequisites of the application of the pleasure principle. Thus we arrive at a conception in which relations to reality are determined by a *reality principle in the broader and a reality principle in the narrower sense* [p. 44].

Such prefigured modes of adaptation to the environment are the principal methods by which genetic information is transformed into behavior in lower animals (Lorenz, 1965). We know that man's essential nature rests upon the fact that rigid stereotypic instinctual modes of adaptation found in other animals are minimal in the human species, but it would be a mistake to believe that such modes do not exist in man. Such mechanisms can be demonstrated most clearly in the earliest developmental period. For example, Spitz' observation of the first social response, the infant's smiling response to his mother's face, is not a piece of learned behavior; it is innate, and analogous to the so-called innate releasing mechanisms observed by ethologists. Similarly, the capacity to differentiate self from object, to distinguish an inside from an outside, to perceive separate objects in physical space, proceeds along a rigidly determined, innate timetable. This does not mean that such processes are uninfluenced by the environment, that is, by the quality of the maternal care. But this is also true of analogous mechanisms in lower animals. The details of this process have been explicated by Piaget's careful observations of the behavior of infants (Piaget, 1954). The fact that the capacity to differentiate the self from other objects in space is not present at the beginning of life does not argue against its being innate. The observation of ethology also demonstrates the gradual acquisition of "structures of adaptation," structures which the environment facilitates or "releases" (Lorenz, 1965). Piaget records well defined stages in the development of the capacity to distinguish self from objects. He concludes that the capacity to "maintain an image" of absent objects is established by the age of 16 to 18 months. Freud described a similar capacity and suggested that the infant's ability to escape from the promptings of instinctual tensions leads to his differentiation of an inner and an outer world. In *Civilization and Its Discontents* Freud (1930) states:

> An infant at the breast does not as yet distinguish his ego from the external world as a source of the sensations flowing in upon him. He gradually learns to do so, in response to various promptings. He must be very strongly impressed by the fact that some sources of excitation, which he will later recognize as his own bodily organs, can provide him with sensations at any moment, whereas other sources evade him from time to time—among them what he desires most of all, his mother's breast—and only to reappear as a result of screaming for help. In this way there is for the first time set over against the ego an 'object,' in the form of something which exists 'outside' and which is only forced to appear by special action [p. 67].

(Freud [1915a] presented essentially the same point of view in an earlier paper, *Instincts and Their Vicissitudes*).

We can now say, making use of Hartmann's terminology, that Freud's description of the infant's gradual acquisition of the capacity to distinguish inside from outside by means of instinctual promptings is autonomous. This autonomous sphere of adaptation to reality that permits the perceptual separations of objects in space must be distinguished from another sphere of reality that we have described in Chapter II, that is, the structuring of reality that is created through need. The relationship between these two spheres is one of the major issues that will be considered in this monograph; in certain instances these two modes of apprehension exist side by side without communication. This is characteristic of certain pathological states and has been described by Freud as a "split in the ego" (Freud, 1927). In the normal individual these two spheres of ego functioning are not separated; the created environment and the autonomously perceived environment interpenetrate.

Our description of the created world of prehistoric man has also been one-sided. We know that he cannot have survived by employing magic alone. Magical thinking creates a world where all objects are interconnected—separateness between the symbol and the object in the environment is not acknowledged. However, from another point of view the physical separateness and "actual" characteristics of objects in space must have been fully acknowledged; and there is good evidence that prehistoric man must have possessed a considerable store of empiric knowledge in order to survive (Singer et al., 1954). Rochlin (1965) discussed this same point.

The Created Environment

We shall now return to another characteristic of Paleolithic art that we noted in passing in the previous chapter. These ancient artists frequently made use of natural geological formations, that is, natural accidents, for their created products. We mentioned earlier that cavities in the rocks were used to represent an animal's wounds. This tendency to utilize the actual earthy structure was quite widespread. For example, in the ceiling of the great hall in Altimara the rounded protuberances of the rock surfaces are covered with paint and transformed into bisons, shown in various postures (Graziosi, 1960). Stalagmitic formations are transformed into a bison rearing up onto its hind quarters. At Niaux a cavity in the rock is used to represent the pupil of a bison's eye. It is not to be supposed that the artists were lacking in imagination so that they required the suggestion of natural forms. In fact, this tendency to make use of the geological structure was a later development of Paleolithic art; had the artists lacked the necessary technical skill, we should expect to find such examples in the earliest stages of this art.

What I shall now suggest as a possible explanation is pure conjecture, but it is a conjecture based on inferences derived from the observation of early mental development. I wish to use this account of Paleolithic art to illustrate a mode of relating to both the inanimate and human environment, the transitional object relationships.

We have previously underscored the fact that the created image in Paleolithic art is not used in a denotive sense but *is* in fact the object in the environment. I would like to suggest that the interpenetration of the actual environment, that is, the walls and ceilings of the cave itself, with the created image, reflects the wish inherent in this art. That is, literally to create the environment. To understand this we must abandon, or attempt to abandon, our adult and contemporary modes of thought. These are not pictures on a wall or on a surface; the images and the surface, that is, the earth, interpenetrate. This is in accord with the belief in the chthonic power of the cave itself, a belief in earth as a generative force. It is the power of the symbol to give form to the environment—to literally create the environment. But what is created is not a hallucination—it has substance, hardness, and permanence.

Winnicott (1951) has observed an analogous process in the young child. By the end of the first year of life the child is able to provide a substitute for its mother that is the result of his own creative illusion. That is, he is able to invest an inanimate object with the qualities of life. Winnicott terms this object a transitional object; it is the child's first possession, the familiar blanket or Teddy bear. This is an object; it is part of the environment; it is something, not a hallucination. According to Winnicott it is a thing created by the infant and at the same time provided by the environment. As with Paleolithic paintings the inner process interpenetrates the objects of the environment and gives them life.

Transitional Object Relationships

Winnicott's observation of the transitional inanimate object of the child—an object that is a substitute for the maternal environment but is itself created, invested with life, a life that is given form by the child's own inner world—is analogous to certain types of adult love relationships.

Human experiences do not lend themselves to rigid schemes of classification—there are no platonic absolutes in human life. In this chapter I shall describe a more primitive form of love relationship, which can be delineated from a more mature form of loving but not delineated in any absolute sense. This more primitive mode of loving and relation to the environment is more characteristic of the borderline and schizophrenic patient than the neurotic (Winnicott, 1945, Modell, 1963).[1] We do not suggest that there is any sharp line of demarcation between the love relationships of the neurotic and psychotic individual, inasmuch as some elements of the transitional object relationship can be discerned in everyone. Freud likened the mind to Rome, the Eternal City, a structure that contains within it the elements of earlier organizations. Freud (1930) states, in *Civilization and Its Discontents,*

> . . . that in mental life nothing which has once been formed can perish—that everything is somehow preserved and that

[1] For reasons that will be discussed later I prefer the term "transitional object relationship" to the more commonly used designation of "symbiotic object relation" or the older term "part object relation."

in suitable circumstances (when, for instance, regression goes
back far enough) it can once more be brought to light [p. 69].

So that this more primitive mode of object relatedness stands
behind the capacity for a more mature form of loving.

We have referred to A. Freud's and Burlingham's observations of young children in wartime for whom the environment is the mother. They experienced no fear of bombing
if their mothers were with them and if their mothers were
unafraid (or did not communicate their fear).[2]

An analogous situation can be observed in the transference
relationship of borderline and schizophrenic patients.[3] In
such individuals the person of the analyst will be regarded as
the protective environment in a manner very much the same
as A. Freud and Burlingham described. The patient believes
that his safety in the world depends only upon the sustained
relationship with the analyst. An illusion is created: as long
as the relationship to the analyst is maintained, the patient
is protected from the dangers of the environment and no
harm can befall him. It is as if the analyst is a shield against
the dangers of the world. Death, disease, aging, limitations
of power, are not real—the only real concern is the relationship with the analyst. This belief can be so extreme that the
patient will actually place his life in danger, secure in the
thought that the analyst will protect him from harm. I described a patient who made a serious suicidal attempt with
a complete denial of the possibility of death; he believed in
my magical abilities to protect him from harm (Modell, 1961).

[2] As Freud noted in *Inhibitions, Symptoms and Anxiety* (1926), the young
child experiences anxiety both in relation to the loss of the protective parental
object and as the result of an internal process—that is, heightened instinctual
claims that threaten the loss of the object.

[3] The transference relationship is, in a certain sense, a magnifying lens, in
that it concentrates reactions but does not create them anew. It is not simply
an artifact of psychoanalytic technique, so that we can, as did Freud, make
inferences concerning object love in general as a result of observing transference love.

As is true with the transitional inanimate object of the child, the transitional human object is an object that stands midway between what is created by the inner world and that which exists in the environment. The transitional object is not completely created by the individual, it is not a hallucination, it is an object "in" the environment. It is something other than the self, but the separateness from the self is only partially acknowledged, since the object is given life by the subject. It is a created environment—created in the sense that the properties attributed to the object reflect the inner life of the subject. The actual characteristics of the analyst's personality, the fact that he is a separate person, with a life and interest of his own, apart from that of the patient, is completely denied. The image of the analyst is created in accordance with need. He exists for them alone. Such a relationship is dyadic, exclusive; this couplet encompasses the entire environment (Hendrick, 1951). This lack of appreciation of the separate qualities of the object leads to a certain exploitive tendency—the object serves only for the gratification of need (A. Freud, 1952) and the subject shows an infant's "preconcern" toward the object (Winnicott, 1945).

Omnipotence and Merging

This creative illusion that denies the sense of separateness between the self and the object is an illusion of action at a distance. As we have observed earlier this is the essence of the concept of magic and omnipotence. In the patient's view, the unlimited power of the therapist is such that he can protect the subject from harm, that is, from the dangers of the "real environment." The patient does not believe that he is "actually in the world" and relinquishes responsibility for himself. He expects the analyst to possess the power to effect a cure; the patient need not work or be active as the analyst will do it for him.

In accordance with the fundamentally ambivalent instinctual attitude of the young child, the relation of the subject
to a transitional object is also fundamentally ambivalent. The
intensity of desire is such that it can never be gratified and
the object is in constant danger of a confrontation with the
subject's unbearable, destructive rage, a rage which is experienced as limitless destruction and which, therefore, needs to
be externalized by means of projection. The analyst's magical power for good may easily be converted to the opposite—
he will appear then as a malevolent sorcerer. This leads to
what has been called the problem of basic trust (Erikson,
1959). Malevolent fantasies are frequently embodied in the
myth that the object is an evil hypnotist who can force his
will upon the helpless and unwilling subject. The belief in
action at a distance is common to both the transitional object relationship and the phenomenon of hypnosis, support-
ing Freud's hypothesis that hypnosis was a primitive form of
loving (Freud, 1921).

If the object is created in accordance with the needs of
the subject, it is not immediately evident why the subject
should wish to terrify himself with the creation of a malevolent object. There is, however, as Freud noted, an adaptive
advantage to eject from the self everything that is bad (Freud,
1925). Freud stated [p. 237], "What is bad, what is alien to the
ego and what is external are, to begin with, identical." This
process of projection is of great adaptive significance. However, the relation to the external object needs to be preserved
at all costs, so that the badness that has been extruded upon it
must be in some manner mitigated. Such fundamental conflicts are resolved by the mental mechanism of splitting. The
creation of a malevolent therapist has a certain adaptive significance; however, the idea of a malevolent therapist cannot be accepted if the patient believes that his safety depends
upon the bond between himself and the therapist. The solu-

tion is to create a dual image in the mind of both an omnipotently good and an omnipotently destructive object. Melanie Klein has described these processes as the "paranoid and depressive position." A critical consideration of these concepts will be reserved for later chapters.

The technical terms that have been used to describe these mental mechanisms are introjection and projection. That is to say, there is a fluidity, an oscillation between what is attributed to the environment and what is taken into the self. To preserve the self, "badness" must be extruded onto the object. However, then the object needs to be preserved, and this is accomplished by means of splitting the object, which is then taken "back into the self," so that the self-image becomes contaminated with the "badness" of the object. The transitional object is not a part of the self—it is "something" in the environment. However, it is endowed with qualities that are created by the subject by the oscillation of introjection and projection. Therefore, the mode of transitional object relationships is one where the differences between the self and the object are minimized. The object is not acknowledged as separate from the self.

It can, therefore, be understood that the experience of merging with the loved object is but a further extension of this process, if the differences between the self and object are already minimized. This fusion, I believe, is implicit whether or not it is consciously experienced. The merging with a "good" object can be experienced as a state of religious mysticism, sexual ecstasy, or a manic denial (Lewin, 1950). Conversely, when there is an intense fear of merging with a "bad" object the subject may fear a loss of identity, a dread of being influenced, and ultimately may fear complete annihilation.[4]

4 Observations of the experience of merging and fusion in borderline and schizophrenic patients were first noted by the pioneering investigations of Federn (1952), who described this process as a "loss of ego boundaries." For a more recent discussion, see Jacobson (1964).

Object Love and Reality

Freud (1930) had noted earlier that the experience of fusion was a form of religious experience in otherwise normal individuals. He recalled that his friend (later identified as Romain Rolland) described in himself the existence of a sensation of "eternity," a limitless, unbounded, "oceanic" feeling. Freud perceived that this experience of merging contained certain elements of the earliest mother-child relationship.

To summarize: belief in omnipotent objects carries with it the implication of belief in action at a distance—there is an implied sense of connectedness, whether or not there is conscious sense of fusion or merging with the object.

The Self as the Environment

The transitional object relationship has been described as analogous to the stage of childhood where the mother *is* the environment for the child, that is, the human object stands between the subject and the dangers of the actual environment. There is in this instance a dependence upon the loved object. This picture has to be modified to include observations which, on the surface, appear to point in an entirely opposite direction. Many individuals characterized as borderline or psychotic do not show such a dependence upon others but instead display a disdainful aloofness. They attempt to create the illusion that they have no need for other human beings—that they are in fact self-sufficient. Such people have been called schizoid.

Now, we have noted earlier that the threat of losing the object arises not only from the possibility of actual physical separation but also from the intensity of instinctual demands made by the subject. These "schizoid" individuals have attempted to solve this conflict by avoiding instinctual demands —that is, they appear as if they need nothing from other human beings. Phases in which there are excessive demands upon a transitional object may alternate in the same individual with the very opposite attitude, or the dependent mode may never be acknowledged.

Jones (1913) described one variant of this character type as the god complex. These people maintain a belief that they are essentially self-sufficient, that they do not need others and indeed, what they have obtained in life has been entirely the result of their own efforts—they are self-created. When one penetrates into this attitude, one discovers a belief that they are in some fashion encapsulated from the dangers of the environment. They "do not really feel in the world." One patient expressed that he felt as if he lived in a plastic bubble. As long as they remain within this bubble they will, they believe, lead a charmed life.

The basis of such an illusion is invariably found to rest upon a belief in their own omnipotence. That is to say, they can be an omnipotent object to themselves; they can provide all the sources of gratification, create their own protective shield against the dangers of the environment. They can be a transitional object to themselves.

It may be asked how such individuals can exist in society if their view of their relations to the world is so primitive. They do, of course, come into conflict with their environment —they are relatively unable to love but they crave admiration. They have spun a magical cocoon around themselves that creates the illusion that they are "not in the real world." A cocoon, no matter how well insulated, needs to be attached to something. These people who crave admiration and deny the need for love usually attach themselves to some other human being, though the significance or importance of this relationship is usually denied or minimized.

The wish to retain this magical illusion, that is, to remain encapsulated from the real world, is a formidable resistance to psychoanalytic treatment. If, after the result of considerable effort, some reduction in the belief of the omnipotence of the self has been achieved, we can regularly observe the emergence of a feeling of intense despair, not unlike the despair to which existential philosophy has addressed itself, a despair that follows the loss of God. It is the despair that results from the acceptance of one's own separateness and helplessness against the dangers that exist in the world.

To summarize our descriptive account of the transitional object relationship: the transitional object is a substitute for the actual environment—a substitute that creates the illusion of encapsulating the subject from the dangers of the environment. The transitional object is not a hallucination— it is an object that does exist "in the environment," separate from the self, but only partially so. It is given form and structure, that is, it is created by the needs of the self. The relationship of the subject to the object is fundamentally ambivalent; the qualities of the object are magical and hence there is an illusion of connectedness between the self and the object. The relation of the subject to the object is primarily exploitive, the subject feels no concern for the needs of the object and cannot acknowledge that the object possesses his own separateness and individuality. The transitional object relationship is dyadic—it admits no others.

A Note on the Term Symbiotic and Part Object Relationship

There is, I believe, greater agreement amongst psychoanalysts concerning the facts of clinical observation than on the terms used to denote those observations. This may be dismissed as a trivial issue. However, the descriptive language of psychoanalysis is derived from theory, and as such the terms employed cannot help but have some influence on the way one thinks about the processes that they denote. What we have been describing as a transitional object relationship is, in a broad sense, equivalent to what has been referred to recently as a symbiotic object relationship. In the older psychoanalytic literature elements of our descriptive account have been referred to as a "part object relationship," and some still adhere to this terminology.

The term "symbiotic relationship" has been widely employed to describe the typical transference relationship of schizophrenic patients and also the child's first object relation (Searles, 1965, and Mahler, 1963). In naming new concepts we find it necessary to fall back upon metaphors and analogies. The symbiotic concept is a metaphor taken from biology. It can be defined as a living together of two species in which both derive advantages therefrom (Zeuner, 1954). It has been appropriately applied to the interaction of the mother and her infant in that both are bound to each other by compelling biologic needs (Benedek, 1949). However, the application of this metaphor to adult love relationships is misleading. The attitude of the subject to the object *may* be analogous to the young infant, but there is no compelling reason to assume that the object of this dyad is bound to the subject in an equivalent manner. That is to say, the subject may create a transitional object of any person who happens to be there. This does not mean that the object chosen for such an investment responds to the subject with the instinctual urges of a nursing mother. The concept of symbiotic object relationship is misleading in that it implies an emotional bond of the object to the subject; the emotional attitude of the object to the subject may be quite irrelevant. That is to say, a transitional object relationship may be established regardless of the attitude of the object. He only needs to be there.

Similarly, the older concept of "part object relationship," introduced by Abraham in 1924, was based upon the early observations of the psychopathology of paranoia. In earlier popular psychoanalytic usage the term referred to a love relationship based only upon instinctual gratification. That is to say, the object was viewed not as a whole individual but as a part, an organ, that gratified. The theoretic origin of the part object concept derives from the theory of instincts prior to the growth of ego psychology, and for that reason is one-sided. Furthermore Glover (1956, p. 18) has cogently criticized this term for its poor logic, noting that "the term 'part object' can be legitimately used as a *descriptive* term only when the subject already recognizes the 'complete' object."

Chapter IV

THE SENSE OF IDENTITY: THE
ACCEPTANCE OF SEPARATENESS

Usually we are unaware of our own identities as we are unaware of our own bodies unless we are ill. However, psychoanalytic investigation has indicated that in some people the
sense of identity is not a silent process; where there is psychopathology, the sense of identity may be a central issue.
Again we must remind the reader that when we differentiate
neurotic from psychotic processes, we are not referring to
sharply defined absolute categories.

In our description of transitional object relations in the
previous chapter we have noted that there is a fluid inter-
change between the qualities of the subject and the qualities
attributed to the object. The transitional object is something
in the environment, but it is invested with the contents of
the subject's own inner world. The sense of self, the sense of
identity, in these individuals appears to be organized about
omnipotent images (Jacobson, 1964). The sense of self is
"self-created." It is not quite accurate to describe an absence
of the sense of self in psychotic individuals; it is rather that
the sense of self is tenuous, as it is organized around the
products of the wish. The sense of identity lacks stability and
coherence. Furthermore, the sense of self is usually perceived
as something negative, degraded, and unwanted. These people do not love or accept themselves.

There are also elements in the self that correspond to an identification with the hated or feared qualities of the parents. So that the self image, such as it does exist, is not completely self-created, but may correspond to certain qualities of the parents' characters that "exist in reality." This is not to say that an identification with feared or hated parents corresponds precisely to the actual qualities of the parents' character; in certain cases one is able to satisfy oneself that the negative qualities attributed to the parental objects are not simply "imagined."

The earliest core of the sense of identity in all individuals is believed to be organized around bodily feelings, especially feelings concerning the genitals (Greenacre, 1958). Freud (1923, p. 26) said that "the ego is first and foremost a bodily ego." In many borderline patients with a negative sense of self we discern that the core of the sense of self is organized around feelings of "defective or dirty" genitals. The sense of self is equated with these feelings and is experienced also as defective and dirty.

It must also be understood that the sense of self, that is, an organization of fantasies concerning the self, may be, to varying degrees, repressed and, therefore, unconscious. Or to state it more precisely, the sense of self which is uncovered during the course of psychoanalytic treatment is an earlier sense of identity, the identity of early childhood, an identity which had once been conscious and then had undergone repression.

To recapitulate: in the psychotic individual there is not an absent sense of self but a sense of self that is unstable, poorly organized, and negative. The content of this sense of identity is magical and self-created, that is, it is organized around highly ambivalent fantasies of omnipotence, and may incorporate fantasies concerning the genitals. It may also contain identifications with the negative qualities of the feared or hated parents.

The disturbance of the sense of identity and its relationship to psychosis was first observed by Helene Deutsch (1942). She observed a group of people who behave "as if" they experience appropriate emotional responses to others. But one learns that they are only acting, that their emotional responses lack depth and genuineness; because of the negative qualities of their actual sense of self they must pretend to be somebody that they are not. Winnicott (1960) has also described a similar phenomenon that he calls "the false self." He noted that the sense of identity in some borderline and schizophrenic people is false in the sense that it is based upon a compliance. The sense of self lacks consistency and permanence so that the individual learns to blend himself, chameleon-like, into the environment and can change his character in accordance with the demands of the environment.

The sense of self or the sense of identity refers to two related aspects—that of sameness amidst flux (Lichtenstein, 1961); and that of individuality—the *unique* configuration of the self.

The psychoanalytic transference provides the medium through which the experience of the patient's sense of self can be constantly observed. Furthermore, psychoanalytic treatment provides a method by which qualitative differences (but not absolute differences) between the neurosis and psychosis may be discerned.

A defective sense of identity in borderline and psychotic individuals is, I believe, a major element in the creation of the qualitatively different transference relationship that occurs in these patients (see also Zetzel, 1956a, 1965a). It is not true, as Freud once believed, that the psychotic remains inaccessible to the psychoanalytic method because he is incapable of forming a transference. For we now know that psychotic people do in fact form a transference relationship of the most intense sort, a transference corresponding to the mode of the transitional object relationship—the person of the analyst becomes a created environment. Some psychotic individuals can be successfully treated provided there are certain modifications in the psychoanalytic method, that is, a period of special preparation is needed. If the underlying diagnosis is unrecognized or if the analyst proceeds to treat the borderline patient as he would a neurotic patient, a deepening overt psychosis may be precipitated. The technical modifications that are employed to treat borderline patients point to the central importance of the sense of identity. For, in order to utilize the technique of classical psychoanalysis, the patient must be able to maintain, in at least a portion of the mind, what has been termed "reality testing," that is, a capacity to maintain judgmental processes that can distinguish the inner world from the outer environment. As we shall describe, *the sense of identity is essential for the testing of reality.*

Although the transference relationship in psychoanalytic treatment is extremely complex and is as yet not fully understood, it is generally agreed that the psychoanalytic method does induce a regression (Zetzel, 1956a). That is to say, the patient reexperiences older aspects of the self—the person of the analyst is experienced in accordance with the images of formerly loved persons that comprised the patient's inner world. According to Nunberg, transference has a Janus-like, two-faced aspect. In one sense it is a repetition of older experiences brought into the present; however, in another sense transference attempts to "reanimate" these "frozen psychic formations, to discharge their energy and to satisfy them in a new and present reality" (Nunberg, 1951, p. 126). One function of transference represents an attempt at mastery through the reawakening of older images, an attempt to master by means of the images of the inner world what had remained unmastered in the ego's relationship to external reality. Here we may refer back to the infant who plays with a spool in order to master his separation from his mother

(see Chapter II). In another sense transference is an attempt
to wrest gratification in the present, to demand instinctual
gratification from the current object, the person of the
analyst.

In both neurosis and psychosis there is a creative aspect in
the perception of the person of the analyst, but there are also
certain essential differences that separate the neurotic from
the psychotic. Despite the regressive alterations, the neurotic
individual (for the most part) does not lose his sense of identity; there is still a portion of himself that maintains some
sense of saneness and continuity. The sense that "I am I"
is maintained. The preservation of this capacity to have
distance from the immediate experience is essential for the
process of analyzing. There is a portion of the neurotic patient's ego that fully apprehends the analyst "as he is." That
is to say, the sense of identity that is maintained in the neurotic patient permits the acceptance of the sense of the
analyst's identity.

We no longer believe that it is essential for the analyst to
be a "blank screen," a "mirror" or "completely neutral."
Contemporary psychoanalysts have come to recognize that in
addition to recognition of the transference relationship, it is
essential that there is an actual human bond between the
therapist and the patient (Stone, 1961). This relation does
not mean friendship, nor a social relationship outside of the
analytic situation, but it does mean that parallel to the transference relationship there is an actual human tie between
the patient "as he is" and the analyst "as he is." Although the
analyst is hidden from the patient's sight, the patient cannot
help but observe, with the passage of time, some aspects of
the analyst's "true" personality. The analyst is not anony-
mous, nor is it desirous for him to be so. It is the aspect of
the actual relationship between the analyst, "as he is," and the
patient, "as he is," that is, the mature portion of the patient's
ego, that forms the working relationship, the therapeutic

alliance, of the analytic process. Without the awareness and acceptance of this "other" relationship, there can be no analysis.

With the borderline or schizophrenic patient their tenuous sense of identity may not be able to withstand the induced regression of the psychoanalytic process. This tenuous sense of identity can be "lost" in a psychotic individual and he may experience the delusion that he has become a different person (Jacobson, 1954). Furthermore, in borderline and psychotic individuals when transference develops they are not able to acknowledge the perceptions of the analyst "as he is." The environment, and this includes the person of the analyst, is created anew in accordance with the needs of the inner world. Knowledge that is gained from perception is disavowed. (This will be discussed more fully in later chapters.) We label this process denial, which may lead to a failure of reality testing, and the transference is then described as a transference psychosis, rather than a transference neurosis. However, we have not gained much from the application of these terms unless we understand what is actually taking place.

I believe that the autonomous functions of the ego, which we noted earlier (Chapter III), are retained. The neurotic and the psychotic individual are both able to *perceive* the analyst "as he is"—to observe his individuality. However, the psychotic patient confines these observations to one portion of his mind, a portion which does not communicate with the other. There is, to follow Freud's metaphor, a split in the ego. There is a failure of connectedness between one portion of the ego and the other, whereas in the neurotic individual there is a greater interpenetration between perceptions of the autonomous ego and perceptions that are essentially self-created.

Consequently, at certain times in his treatment the psychotic patient may not acknowledge that the analyst is a relatively benign individual who is only trying to help; he may be perceived instead as a malevolent hypnotist, intent on destroying the patient. The fact that he is a physician and that the patient has come to him for treatment, is completely denied. The ambient transference has substituted another reality.

In order to minimize the development of a psychotic transference, various modifications of the usual psychoanalytic technique have been introduced. In general these modifications have as their aim the strengthening of the patient's perceptions of the analyst "as he is" and the strengthening of the analyst's perception of the patient "as he is." Although there is not universal agreement on this point, analysts in this country tend, at least at the beginning of treatment of borderline and schizophrenic patients, to avoid the use of the psychoanalytic couch and to sit facing the patient. What is essential here is the fact that the patient can see the *analyst's* face. It is not only that the patient has an added opportunity to perceive the unique qualities of the analyst. My experience which corresponds to that of others (Searles, 1965) has convinced me that what is more important is the fact that the patient can see the analyst reacting to *him,* as a unique person. This observation suggests that the earliest sense of identity may be induced by the experience of the child perceiving its mother's face responding to it. The child sees itself reflected in its mother's face (Spitz, 1965). It is essential for the analytic treatment of both the neurotic and psychotic patient, but especially the psychotic patient, that the analyst perceive the patient not as an "it" but as a "thou." That is, the analyst must be able to perceive the patient's uniqueness and individuality and to respond with genuine feeling (although not necessarily expressed) to the patient's genuine feeling. It is not only essential for the analytic process that the patient perceive the analyst's uniqueness, but that the patient perceive the analyst perceiving him; the patient's own sense of identity is strengthened by observing the analyst reacting to him as an individual.

Psychoanalysis and the Concept of Identity

Psychoanalysts' recent interest in the sense of identity is a result of knowledge they have gained from treating borderline and schizophrenic patients. It is a concept that is derived from observation, not from theoretical preconceptions.

However, the sense of self, the sense of identity, is also a religious concept, one embedded in an entirely different intellectual tradition. The concept of self in this sense is very ancient and not completely divorced from magical thinking. It forms a central feature in Indian philosophy. The self (Atman) is that which is eternal and everlasting (Zimmer, 1951). The self is ageless, eternal but also substantial. The search for the self, that is, a period of self-observation and withdrawal, occupies the third and fourth stages of life, according to the Hindu religion. After one has achieved one's material needs, one retreats and searches for the "true self." The concept of self in this religious sense has some relation to magical ideas, in that it contains the notion of permanence and indestructiveness, that is, it is a negation of the reality of separation and death.

The concept of idiosyncratic individuality is alien to Eastern thought. Eastern philosophy, however, does acknowledge the difference between the "true" and "false" self. The personality that one shows to the world is, to the Hindu, a mask —the true eternal self remains hidden. The mask may be dropped upon the death of the body, but the true self survives and is later reincarnated (Zimmer, 1951). As Zimmer notes, this idea of the self has some relation to the Christian notion of the soul.

The concept of personality as a mask to be discarded is alien to Western thought. Yet there is something here that has been adopted by Western psychology, or rather imported into Western psychology by Jung. Jung has employed the term "persona" in its literal sense as denoting the social face that is presented to the world, in contrast to the true self that remains hidden. The etymology of the English word "personality" suggests a relation to the Eastern concept of the persona in that "personality" was originally derived from the Latin "persona" (*per sonat*), the mask through which the actor sounds his part (Zimmer, 1951, and Oxford English Dictionary). This is a reference to the mask worn by actors in the Greek, and later Roman, drama.

The fact that Jung adapted Indian philosophy for his own purposes and introduced the terms "persona" and "individuation," whereas Freud did not concern himself with the concept of identity, has led some Freudian analysts to attack the entire current interest in the concept of identity as a Jungian epiphenomenon (Glover, 1966).

In the psychological sense, as opposed to the religious, the sense of identity is the result of a psychic structure, the product of a developmental process of the ego (for a critical review of recent psychoanalytic concepts of identity, see Jacobson, 1964). We can conceptualize the sense of identity as a structure within the ego (Hartmann, 1939), or as an ego substructure. The term "self" is not equivalent to the idea of the ego as a whole, as is true in religious thought. We may tentatively describe the sense of identity as the result of a functional organization within the ego—having its origin in successive nodal periods of development. (Theoretical problems concerned in this concept will be described in Chapters VIII and IX.) The sense of identity is the result of a synthetic activity of the ego. There are, of course, many senses of identity, originating in successive developmental phases, that persist alongside of or underneath the development of a more mature sense of identity. The earliest sense of identity consists of a composite of omnipotent fantasies combined with early images of the body. This structure is continually enriched and remodeled, especially at crucial points in development such as the early oedipal period, puberty, and adolescence (Erikson, 1959, Jacobson, 1964). But the search for identity does not end with adolescence. The poet, Auden, believes, and we concur, that we do not know who we are until after the age of forty. Identity here is used in Erikson's sense of finding one's place in society, of seeing oneself "objectively" in relation to other men. In a certain sense Western society has become obsessed with the theme of identity, the search for uniqueness. This may be seen most clearly in contemporary art, in contrast to former periods, when artists could identify themselves as adherents to a style or a school; today each artist strives only for individual expression.

What Erikson (1959) has described as a search for identity —finding one's identity in relation to social groups—is a process of exploring social realities through group identifications. It is an enlarging of social judgments, so that ultimately individual judgment, the ability to see oneself "as one is," cannot be separated from the capacity to identify with others. It is a sharing of group judgments; the individual finds his own identity in relationship to the community's response. The group now performs the function once attributed to the mother. Erikson states:

> Identity formation, *finally*, begins where the usefulness of identification ends. It arises from the selective repudiation and mutual assimilation of childhood identifications, and their absorption in a new configuration, which in turn is dependent on the process by which a *society* (often through sub-societies) identifies the young *individual*, recognizing him as somebody who had to become the way he is, and who, being the way he is, is taken for granted [Erikson, 1959, p. 113].

Identification and the Failure of Identification

We have described individuals whose development was arrested at the stage of transitional object relations, who have a poorly developed sense of identity, and who still rely on others, as does the young child, to protect them from the dangers of the environment. And we have contrasted this group to others whose development has proceeded past the stage of transitional object relations—those who are capable of a more mature love. How is this arrest in development to be understood?

What follows cannot be a definitive answer but is, nevertheless, a firm impression based upon clinical observation. Let us start by considering a process that is more familiar to us—Freud's description of the formation of the superego (Freud, 1923). Before the child develops his own conscience (I have attempted elsewhere to differentiate the experience of primitive guilt from the formation of the definitive superego [Modell, 1965]), he is in part dependent upon the external world, that is, his parental objects, to control his impulses. Later, when the superego or conscience becomes part of his psychic apparatus, the child will be able to perform for himself those functions of restraint previously assigned to parental objects. Freud described that a "piece of the external world" had been internalized.

Freud understood this process to be the outcome of identifications with parental objects, particularly the father. By this means the content of the parent's superego and, in a general sense, the attitudes of society, become part of the internal world of the child. As Freud recognized, this is a process of momentous significance. The identification permits an instinctual renunciation—the male child, by means of his identification with his father, is enabled to modify his sexual claims upon his mother.

In the more than 40 years since *The Ego and the Id* was

written, psychoanalytic knowledge has deepened to include a fuller understanding of an equally momentous stage of development that precedes the formation of the definitive superego. It is, as Freud said, analogous to the discovery of the prehistoric Mycenaean culture that preceded Greek civilization (Freud, 1930).

We now know that identifications do not originate in the oedipal period but are established much earlier, prior to the third year of life. For certain people a disturbance during this developmental period may prove to be decisive.

The development of the first core of the sense of identity occurs in this earlier period and represents a process analogous in certain respects to the later formation of the definitive superego. Here too there is a "taking in" to the ego of a function that was once attributed to parental objects, that is, a portion of the external world is internalized. I have described the stage of transitional object relations as one where the individual believes, as does a young child, that his safety in the world depends upon the presence of protective parent surrogates. There is here a failure to assimilate an executive function into the ego—a failure to take something in.

Hendrick (1951) observed an earlier stage of ego formation that precedes the development of the definitive superego. He described an early ego identification that is the consequence of the quality of the *actual* object relation with the mother. He described an identification with the mother's way of doing things that leads to an internalization of certain executant capacities, which increases the child's capacity to deal effectively with the external world. Hendrick's hypothesis has been confirmed by direct child observation (Ritvo and Solnit, 1958).

In our description of the sense of identity in borderline patients we noted that there is an absence of a feeling of a "beloved self." The developmental histories of these patients almost uniformly reveal a disturbance in the *actual* relationship between themselves and their mothers in the first and second years of life. There is evidence of a failure of this early maternal environment, a failure to provide what Winnicott has called "good enough" maternal care. The relative failure of the maternal environment is suggested not only by a reconstruction of the patient's early life history but also by the more direct observation of the transference relationship. These people are inordinately sensitive to any sign of the analyst's less than absolute reliability. That is, a slight inconsistency, such as a change in appointment, a lateness or a missed hour, may be experienced as an immediate threat of complete abandonment. Winnicott (1962), has interpreted this response (and my own experience and that of many colleagues confirms his observations) as evidence of the fact that the psychoanalytic relationship is a "holding environment" for the patient. It provides certain elements of reliability and constancy that the patient did not receive in the first years of life.

The term "holding" also suggests something else: parents provide not only love but also restraint. The infant, in a state of rage, needs to be held. Parents are not only a source of love but also facilitate impulse control. This is not only at the stage of the formation of the definitive superego—presumably between the ages of three and five—but also at earlier stages as well. Although we cannot discuss these developmental processes in detail, it is evident that there are certain critical stages that require a specific "fitting in" of the environment, a "fitting in" that is provided for by the quality of the parental object relationships. Human beings have, fortunately, in most instances, two parents, so that there is a certain margin of safety—the failure of one parent may be rectified by the resources of the other.

The persistence of the transitional form of object relations in borderline and schizophrenic patients can be traced to this specific failure. We noted that these patients have not identified with a loving and "controlling" parent and hence remain slavishly dependent upon external objects to perform certain functions that have not been incorporated into their own egos. Identifications with parental objects in these instances are either the creation of the subject—identifications based upon the projection of malevolent omnipotence—or identifications with the negative, frightening, or painful qualities of the parental objects—qualities which may be real or imagined.

There has been a failure to incorporate the "good object." This terminology, however, is confusing; we wish to distinguish "the good object" created by the subject to deal with ambivalence—i.e., the idealized object—from a good object that results from a "good enough" object relationship. In this latter instance, the good object cannot be created by the subject; the quality of the identification with the object is determined by the quality of the actual object relation.[1]

To recapitulate: psychic development requires a specific form of identification that depends upon the actual experience of "good enough" parental care. Historical reconstruction does not permit us to date precisely when this identification has occurred; it is a period prior to the development of the definitive superego, that is, prior to the ages of three to five.

Freud noted that the formation of the superego (the identification with parental objects) permits a partial renunciation of the instinctual demands made upon these objects. Identification serves in some way to bind, modify or "neutralize" instinctual demands—it leads to a "taming" of the instincts. The failure of identification in borderline and schizophrenic patients leads to the persistence of crude instinctual attitudes. We can regularly observe in these people

---

[1] Hartmann (1953, p. 191) has described the "good" object as the "constant" object which promotes energy neutralization.

an enormously heightened intensity of sadistic impulses. In some instances the degree of infantile sadism is so great as to be nearly unmodifiable by later experience; it precludes the ability to identify with "good objects" which is the basis of learning. The interaction of ego development and environmental gratification is circular—they are mutually reinforcing. The absence of "good enough" mothering results in a heightened sadistic attitude which, in turn, prevents the process of "taking in" something "good" from the environment should the environmental situation improve.

This failure of identification has other serious consequences. The individual remains helplessly dependent upon the environment; loss of the object results in actual dread of disintegration. Anxiety is total, experienced as a feeling of annihilation. This is in contrast to those who have had "good enough" parental care and who have internalized a "good object." In the latter, anxiety is experienced in a more modulated form and can be tolerated. What is true for anxiety is also true for guilt. Guilt in the borderline and schizophrenic patient does not tend to be circumscribed—it is total, paralyzing, and requires immediate talion punishment (Modell, 1965). I have described a group of borderline or near borderline patients who suffer from intense envy of others— they literally wish to take away everything anyone else has. Consequently, they feel that they are not entitled to have anything for themselves. These patients are understandably extremely difficult to treat, for they feel they do not deserve a better life (see also Zetzel, 1965b).

The experience of a "good enough" holding environment in these early years is necessary for the modulation of those instinctual demands that are made upon the environment. The failure to internalize a "good enough" object also results in the failure to tolerate guilt and anxiety. In other words: the failure of the environment to provide an adequate object relationship at a critical period leads to a failure of ego maturation.[2]

These observations are analogous to the observations of ethology. There are critical periods in development during which there is a specific need for a "fitting in" of the behavior of other objects in the environment (Lorenz, 1965).

We have observed that in some instances this failure of identification is reversible. A successful psychoanalytic treatment can provide in part the experience of "good enough" parental care, and an identification with the analyst can become a permanent part of the patient's ego, thus permitting further ego maturation. In some cases the faulty, negative, or defective sense of identity of borderline and psychotic patients can be repaired. If such a process is successful, it leads to the development of a more definitive self-image and the capacity to form more mature love relations. In others this does not occur. It is as if the failure of the environment at a critical phase has proved to be decisive.

We are not yet able to account fully for these differences, though I have the impression that the degree of sadism, and consequently the need for talion punishment, may prove to be a determinant factor. These patients whose sadism is overwhelming, who do not possess some capacity for love or tender regard for others, remain unable to take in "something good" from the environment. They are unable to form new identifications and in a larger sense are unable to profit from experience. To learn from others and the capacity to love others are at bottom similar; both are based on the capacity to identify. Without this capacity there is no possibility of psychic growth. The processes of knowing and loving have hidden connections that have not as yet been fully appreciated.

[2] Hendrick (1936) also noted that the process of identification would normally terminate intense infantile sadism.

The Sense of Identity and the Acceptance of Limitations

The cohesive sense of identity in the adult is a sign that there has been a "good enough" object relationship in the earliest period of life. Something has been taken in from the environment that has led to the core of the earliest sense of identity, a core which permits further ego maturation.

That a loving parent has been internalized and become part of the self, so that one is able to love oneself, has been described as an aspect of narcissism. The term "narcissism" appears to have acquired unduly negative connotations, for there is, as Waelder (1960) has noted, a positive or adaptive aspect to narcissism. I am suggesting that the awareness of the self as a discrete and beloved entity (the narcissistic gratification of self-love) may enable the individual to accept the fact that objects in the external world are separate and can be lost and destroyed. (See also Rochlin, 1965). This may be nothing more than the old adage that to love others one must first be able to love oneself. Whether or not this assumption is correct, it is a fact that *those individuals who have the capacity to accept the separateness of objects are those who have a distinct, at least in part, beloved sense of self*. If one can be a loving parent to oneself, one can more readily accept the separateness of objects. This is a momentous step in psychic development.

This leads to at least a partial acceptance of the limitation of other objects and of reality. Freud has discussed this process in terms of the transformation of the pleasure principle into the reality principle, and we shall return to a discussion of this issue in Chapter VI. The establishment of this early positive core of the self permits a partial reduction in the need for omnipotence, a partial acceptance of the separateness of objects.

The sense of identity develops episodically; it is never a final process. It grows by accretion during critical life phases.

With each subsequent development in the sense of identity there is a new relationship to external objects and to the environment. With each subsequent deepening development of the sense of identity there is an ever-increasing capacity to accept the limitations of others. However, this process is not to be thought of as final and complete—separateness can never be fully accepted. One may relinquish belief in one's own omnipotence, but belief in an unlimited power may be preserved as an "ego ideal"—something to be achieved in the future. Limitations of the present life may be accepted if one can believe in a future paradise. Similarly, the acceptance of the limitations of parental objects is gradual and painful, but belief that there are *some* omnipotent objects persists. Religion has heretofore provided the institutional structure for the gratification of this wish. And it may be that the loss of religious belief has placed on contemporary man a special strain on the process of identity, leading to an obsessive preoccupation with the problem of identity.

With the partial acceptance of the limitations of other persons and an acceptance of separateness, there is established a capacity for a more mature form of loving, that is, a love relationship that can be maintained in the face of privation and ambivalence. The philosopher Buber has expressed this difference between immature and mature love as the difference between the I-It relation and the I-Thou relation (Buber, 1958). The I-It relationship places things in categories; the I-Thou relationship appreciates the unique, specific qualities of the beloved, qualities that defy classification.

> But love is between I and Thou. The man who does not know this, with every being know this, does not know love; even though he ascribes to it the feelings he lives through, experiences, enjoys, and expresses. Love ranges in its effect through the whole world. In the eyes of him who takes his stand in love, and gazes out of it, men are cut free from

their entanglement in bustling activity. Good people and evil, wise and foolish, beautiful and ugly, become successfully real to him; that is, set free. They step forth in their singleness, and confront him as Thou (Buber, 1958, pp. 14-15).

Buber's definition of loving emphasizes the apperception of the uniqueness of the object, its "real" qualities. The capacity to love, according to Buber, is allied to the capacity to perceive reality. Psychoanalysts would state that to love maturely one must accept the *separateness* of the object.

Love relationships, based upon the acceptance of separateness, may, as they do in the analytic situation, involve the attribution to the object of qualities that are created by the subject. The essential difference between this more mature form of loving and the transitional object relationship is there is an acceptance of knowledge of the object that is gained through perception. That is, there is an interpenetration or intercommunication between knowledge gained from perception of the object "as he is" and qualities attributed to the object by the subject. In transitional object relations the object's individuality is denied. He is there, but he is created by the subject—his own separate identity is disavowed.[3]

Love and Merging

We wish to emphasize that the acceptance of separateness, as is true for the establishment of one's identity, is never absolute or final. Even if one has established the capacity for mature love, established a sense of identity, and accepted the uniqueness of his beloved—there is a wish to merge, to

---

[3] I. Singer (1966) has described love in similar terms. He uses the concept of appraisal and bestowal. Bestowal would correspond to the creation of the object by the subject, whereas appraisal is acknowledgment of the real attributes of the object.

fuse, to lose one's separateness. The lover creates an image of his beloved that arises from his own inner world. It is in one sense a projection of part of himself. There is a reciprocal process on the part of the beloved. It is as if the process of loving consists of the mingling and sharing of psychic substances; what the lover attributes to the beloved he takes back into himself by means of an identification. Despite the acceptance of the separateness of his beloved, the process of loving always contains an element of connectedness.

Plato acknowledges this in his famous myth of the origin of love (quoted by Freud in *Beyond the Pleasure Principle,* 1920, p. 57) that he attributes to Aristophanes in the *Symposium.* There were originally three sexes. There was man, woman, and a union of the two. Primeval man was round, his back and sides forming a circle; he had four hands and four feet, one head with two faces and two privy members. They were split apart by Zeus who wanted to humble them and to diminish their strength. Homosexual love and the love between the sexes are thus explained as the search for the missing half. This ancient myth is testimony to the poet's marvelous insight that fusion represents an older form of loving that is never fully relinquished and that separateness is a form of punishment.

Chapter V

SOME PRE-FREUDIAN CONCEPTS OF "INNER" AND "OUTER" REALITY

The idea of "reality" can only have been formed when the distinction between subject and object was accepted. The cultural achievement represented by this acceptance provided the psychological basis for the origin of scientific thought— an emergence from an animistic world view. As we have suggested, there are certain parallels between psychological processes in the individual that permit acceptance of separateness and analogous processes that lead to changes in social institutions. As Freud indicated in *Group Psychology* and in *Totem and Taboo,* cultural history is antecedent to individual history.

The emergence of a scientific or a prescientific world view, a view that accepts some limitations of human thought recognizes that the environment cannot be moved by wish alone, has been traced to two major cultural traditions—the Greek and the Hebrew (Frankfort et al., 1949, and Von Weizsacker, 1964.) I believe that it is not fortuitous that both Hebrew and Grecian cultures are distinguished from their contemporary and neighboring civilizations by a unique attitude towards the individual. Early Hebrew and Greek society recognized individuality. The notion of individuality is so much a part of our own civilization that it is difficult for us to imagine a time when even the idea of distinguishing the character of individual men was an incredible novelty. All cultures have extolled the exploits of "supermen" in epic poems, but that is not the same thing as a recognition of individuality. We have noted in Chapter IV that the Hindu concept of personality does not contain the idea of individuality—personality is a social mask; the individual is assigned his role by society; the face he presents to the world is of little consequence for it will be discarded after death. The term *persona* in Indian thought must imply that people only impersonate what they seem to be; personality is but the mask of one's part in the comedy or tragedy of life and is not to be identified with the actor (Zimmer, 1951).

If one examines the evidence of iconography and compares Greek with Egyptian sculpture, differences in the attitude towards individuality become clearer. The frieze taken from the Parthenon (now in the British Museum) transmits the Greeks' intoxication with the discovery of individuality. Each figure—horseman, girl, heifer—is captured in characteristic and individualized motion.[1] Contrast this art with the stereotype representation of Egyptian laborers taken from an Egyptian tomb relief, each one resembling the other.

Egyptian art is in the main stylized; figures are produced, with few exceptions, in accordance with conventional formulas. Each figure resembles the other with monotonous regularity (Gombrich, 1960). There are exceptions in the

[1] I am aware that art historians usually attribute to the Greeks an idealization of form which would be inconsistent with the view that Greek art expresses the discovery of individuality. I believe, however, that a truer account of the meaning of Greek art was provided by Gombrich (1960), who compared it with the Egyptian and discovered that it was revolutionary in its function. Egyptian art cannot be separated from its magical religious function; the figures depicted were analogous to the conventionalized figures of chessmen, that is, the form could vary within certain limits but the meaning assigned to the symbol was fixed. Greek art was revolutionary in that it attempted to portray the image in the mind of the beholder. The interest in the human form, especially the nude, is an expression of interest in *individual* bodies. Contrast this to the Egyptians, who were keen observers of animals but were satisfied with conventional stereotypes of the human figure.

funereal portraiture of the privileged classes, where there is an attempt to depict individual facial characteristics. But this art form is connected with the ritualistic function of assuring life after death and does not indicate the discovery of the concept of individuality.

Iconographic evidence cannot be applied to the Hebrews, as the production of graven images was forbidden. If, however, we employ a literary source, the Old Testament, we can discern in the descriptions of Abraham, Isaac, Jacob, Moses, and the prophets a sense of individuality and character. The delineation of a sense of character finds the most complete expression in the Book of Job.

Hebrew thought created a momentous advance over the animistic views held in neighboring Near Eastern countries. In both Egypt and Sumer no distinction was made between nature and gods. In Sumer the primordial ocean *was* the female god, Ti Amat. In Egypt this primeval ocean was male —the god Nūn (Frankfort et al., 1949). "The dominant tenet of Hebrew thought is the absolute transcendence of God. Yahweh is not in nature. Neither earth nor sun nor heaven is divine; even the most potent natural phenomena are but reflections of God's greatness" (Frankfort et al., 1949).

Separating nature from the living god opened an intellectual path which eventually led to the development of scientific thought (Von Weizsacker, 1964). Belief in a transcendental, ineffable god became the bridge between animism and scientific thought.

I suggest that in the development of both the individual and culture the sense of identity permits the acceptance of a separateness from the environment—the acceptance of inanimate nature. Greek and Hebrew society did not, of course, relinquish a belief in mythical or magical thought. But the influence of this form of thought was limited. The relative helplessness of man, that is, his inability to control the environment, was acknowledged by the Greeks and de-

picted as a belief in Moira—implacable fate. The fate of a
Greek individual may be influenced by his relationship to his
gods, as Job's fate was determined by his relationship to his
god—but there is in both instances an acceptance of limitations. There is an obvious analogy to be drawn from the
individual in our own culture who does accept the limitations of his own omnipotence but must continue to believe
that someone is omnipotent. This is true even amongst those
who cease to believe in religion. For in the final stages of
most psychoanalyses one discovers that the patient still clings
to the belief that the analyst is in some way without limitations, and it is only with the greatest reluctance that he accepts the fact that *no one* is omnipotent.

Although magical thought was not by any means absent in
early pre-Platonic Greek thinking (Pythagorean thought, for
example, is steeped in myth), the Greeks did achieve what
Frankfort called a "breathtaking change of viewpoint"—
they achieved an *acceptance of the distinction between subject and object.* Implicit in such an acceptance is the distinction between an inner and outer world—a distinction that
encompasses the differences between subjective and objective
knowledge.

The reader may at this point be wondering why a psychoanalyst attempts to deal at all with these philosophic
issues. One could take the position that philosophers and
psychoanalysts occupy different conceptual worlds—that the
"philosophical" concept of reality is not the psychoanalytic
concept of reality and that the problem of reality and reality
testing as applied to psychological issues is something apart
from the philosophical problems of reality and appearance
and the problems of epistemology. However, whether will-
ingly or not, the psychoanalyst shares with the philosopher
certain ingrained metaphysical assumptions concerning the
nature of reality. Although Freud created psychoanalysis, he
did not create anew all of his intellectual assumptions; no

man can do that. He was influenced, as we all are, by certain ways of looking at the world which may be said to be unspoken metaphysical assumptions whose origins can be traced to certain philosophical traditions.

Psychoanalytic theory has incorporated uncritically, perhaps unknowingly, certain concepts that have their origins in earlier philosophical traditions. The concept of "the representation of objects," for example, can be traced directly to John Locke and an antiquated sensationalist psychology. It is also important for psychoanalysts as well as psychiatrists to know that the problem of reality testing, that is, the capacity to distinguish what is perceived from what is imagined, is an ancient problem. Attempts to solve this problem have engaged some of the best minds in Western civilization, and these attempts have molded Western thought. Psychoanalysis as a body of thought shares certain of these traditions.

It is beyond my competence to trace, however superficially, the history of this thought. I wish only to clarify certain concepts which have become part of the basic assumptions of Freud's psychoanalytic psychology.

It is also important for us to consider to what extent psychoanalysis offers a solution to these ancient problems.

Plato

Most scholars attribute to Parmenides (circa 450 B.C.) the first acknowledgment of the problem of appearance and reality. But it is Plato's philosophy that has had the most enduring influence upon Western thought. Platonic metaphysics still influences even contemporary biology. Mayr (1963), for example, noted that the concept of typology of species in biology had been influenced by the Platonic idea of an absolute universal type corresponding to an "ultimate" reality. Observations of the variation of the species would be interpreted by such modern Platonists as mere appearances. Such a belief in absolute Platonic typologies has influenced psychiatric nosology as well.

Plato was not a psychologist in the modern sense. Although he was fully aware of the problem of the distinction between the observer and that which is observed, he discounted the importance of psychological processes as such, that is, the processes of perception and sensation. These were for Plato mere appearances, as he expresses in the famous simile of the cave (*Republic,* Book VII). Plato asks us to imagine men who are prisoners in a cave with their backs to a fire facing a wall. Of the external world they know only the shadows. If a man should succeed in escaping from this imprisonment into the sun, he would be dazzled by the "real objects." What he had accepted previously as reality were mere shadows. For Plato, sensation and perception were similar to the shadows on the cave wall; ultimate reality consists of the form of ideas—the category of a class of objects that has an enduring existence outside of the apprehending mind. For example (provided by Russell, 1948), man sees an individual cat which partakes in some manner in the nature of *the* ultimate cat which is created by God. *The* cat is real; particular cats are only apparent.

I do not believe that Plato's theory of ideas was incorporated as a hidden assumption into psychoanalytic theory. Yet it is important for us to note that the problems with which we are still struggling, the distinction between imagination and "reality," were recognized as significant problems by Plato, although his solution strikes us as unpsychological, or, to put it more fairly, prepsychological.

Descartes and the Concept of Mind

Descartes was not the first to acknowledge the distinction between subject and object. This distinction was, as we described in the earlier paragraphs, implicit in Greek thought. But, as we have noted, for Plato perception was an epiphenomenon not considered to be significant. Descartes was, therefore, in a certain sense the first modern psychologist, in that he acknowledged the importance of the perceiver. It is to Descartes that we owe the dualism of mind and matter as well as that of mind and body. Modern psychology, and this includes psychoanalysis, still adheres to this distinction between the objects of the material world (*res extensa*) and the psychological objects "of the mind" (*res cogitans*). From one point of view post Cartesian philosophy is the history of a constant attempt to break down these separate realms. Although Ryle (1949) refers contemptuously to Descartes' "myth" as "the dogma of the Ghost in the Machine" and Von Bertalanffy (1964) has attacked the Cartesian mind-body dualism for creating insoluble problems for psychosomatic medicine, we still adhere with some modifications to Descartes' metaphysical assumptions. Psychoanalysis still adheres to the idea that observations obtained by means of its method attain significance by relating these observations to processes "in the mind."[2]

For Descartes, psychological knowledge was the only knowledge of which there is certainty.

> While we thus reject all that of which we can possibly doubt, and feign that it is false, it is easy to suppose that there is no God, nor heaven, nor bodies, and that we possess neither hands, nor feet, nor indeed any body; that we cannot in the same way conceive that we who doubt these things are not; for there is a contradiction in conceiving that what thinks does not at the same time as it thinks, exist. And hence this conclusion I THINK THEREFORE I AM is the first and

[2] In a recent discussion Home (1966) correctly notes that psychoanalysis is a psychology of mind but draws the incorrect inference that psychoanalysis cannot, therefore, be scientific. As it is concerned exclusively with meaning, it is, he believes, a branch of the humanities.

most certain of all that occurs to one who philosophizes in an orderly way (Descartes, *Principles of Philosophy*, Principle vii).

Unfortunately for the growth of psychological science, the method of Descartes' psychology was restricted to that of introspection. This has led to the belief among some philosophers that the mind can only be known by its own possessor, and philosophers still debate the question whether one mind can have knowledge of another mind. Freud was not deterred by this kind of philosophizing. Koestler (1964) noted that if Descartes had been able to include the unconscious mind in his method of introspection, he might have advanced the study of psychology by several hundred years. According to Descartes, mental processes are *private* data. There are still many philosophers who ignore the discoveries of psychoanalysis and continue to believe that "private" data cannot be known by other minds. Bertrand Russell, for example, defines psychology in this ancient Cartesian sense as the sphere of private data—he defines as mental whatever we may know without inference. A public datum is one which "generates similar sensations in all participants and may be observed by many people provided they are suitably placed" (Russell, 1948). Russell, then, adhering to the introspectionist view of mind, does not believe that Freud could have made a science of dream interpretation because we cannot know what a man dreams but only what he says he dreams. It is true that the psychoanalyst cannot know the dream as it is dreamed by the dreamer; there is, in this sense, something that is known by the individual without inference, which corresponds to Russell's definition of private data. However, the psychoanalyst can *make inferences* concerning the function of the dream by means of the dreamer's association even though he is not able to share in the dreamer's dream experience and be certain that the dream reported is the dream as it was actually dreamed.

Freud (1900, p. 512) had anticipated this objection. He answered that, in accordance with the principle of psychic determinism, the remembering of dreams and the recounting of dreams is not arbitrary—that the associations will lead the observer back to the latent content of the dreams regardless of whether the dreamer reports the dreams as they have actually occurred. In this instance the psychoanalyst is treating the dream, a private datum, as if it were a public datum. While psychoanalysis adheres to the distinction between subject and object, between mind and matter, Freud has demonstrated to the world that it is only man's pride that leads him to state that *his* thoughts are the *only* things that can be known with certainty. It is painful for man to acknowledge that this is not true, that even his thoughts cannot be known with certainty, as they are in part unconscious.

Descartes believed that certain thoughts were innate and we shall return to this issue later in this chapter. The correspondence of ideas to the realities outside of the mind was guaranteed, according to Descartes, by the hypothesis of an omnipotent and benevolent God who has fashioned our mind to represent the realities outside of the mind (Barrett, 1962). In this sense man shares an omnipotence borrowed from God, although he has thus partially acknowledged a limitation of his own omnipotence.

Locke and the Concept of the Object Representation

Although Locke took exception to Descartes' belief in the existence of innate ideas, he did perpetuate the Cartesian dualism of mind and matter. An examination of Locke's psychology, especially his concept of the representation of physical objects in the mind, is important, as certain elements of his representational psychology have been retained within the body of psychoanalytic thought and need to be expunged.

Locke adhered, as had Descartes, to the method of introspection, which method was in turn evolved from the method

of self-reflective examination of the religious school men who
had preceded them. By this method he hoped to achieve a
science of mind that would rival the achievements of the
natural sciences. Physics had described elementary particles
of matter, atoms, from which a more complex description of
the physical world can be derived. In an analogous fashion
Locke proposed that we consider that "simple ideas" were
the "atoms" of psychological science. That is, from these
simple ideas we would be able to derive the understanding of
the more complex structures of the mind (Locke, "An Essay
concerning Human Understanding"). You will recall that
Descartes believed that the correspondence between ideas in
the mind and objects in the external world was guaranteed by
the existence of an omnipotent God. The mind, for Descartes,
was essentially a passive receptacle. Despite Locke's disagreement with Descartes concerning the existence of innate ideas,
he retained essentially a passive image of mind with his famous metaphor of the mind as a waxed tablet. In order to
explain the correspondence between objects in the mind and
their counterparts in physical space, Locke did not invoke
Descartes' explanation of a benevolent God who does not play
tricks on his subjects; instead he emphasized the motive
power of the objects in the physical world to induce corresponding ideas in the mind.

> Particles emanating from material objects strike the human
> sense organs setting up a chain of effects in the nervous sys-
> tem, which somehow finally produce an entity different in
> kind from themselves—an idea in the mind [taken from a
> discussion by I. Berlin, 1956].

Locke did not conceive the mind to be entirely passive, in
that he did acknowledge certain active powers—it can combine several "simple" ideas to form a new, compound idea.
Further, he introduced the concept of the association of
ideas which was to become so important in later psychology.

This implies a certain activity of the mind. Although such activity on the part of the subject is acknowledged, it is minimized, as the more complex ideas can ultimately be traced to simple ideas—ideas which were impressed upon the mind by particles emanating from external objects.

His psychology can be described as atomistic sensationalism, a belief that there is a *simple* correspondence between physical objects and their representation in the mind. These object representations are fundamental entities analogous to the elementary particles of the physical world.

These concepts, although they may seem quaint, have had a remarkable longevity. They have been perpetuated by the British philosophical tradition and from this root have been incorporated to some degree into Freud's theory of psychoanalysis. It may be ironic that Freud, who, more than any other man, destroyed the arid introspectionistic psychology that preceded him, has retained at least in small measure certain modes of thought from this earlier tradition. This simply attests to the influence of one's early education; the intellectual baggage that one acquires cannot be completely discarded. Freud's use of Locke's concept of the object representation is most explicit in his paper *The Unconscious* (Freud, 1915b), a theoretical contribution of the highest importance. In this essay Freud attempts to delineate the differences between the major psychological systems of the mind—the conscious, preconscious, and unconscious. Using the psychology of schizophrenia for illustrative purposes, Freud makes a distinction between the verbal "presentation of an object" (*vorstellung*, in the original German), a function of the system preconscious, and a "thing presentation," that is, a function of the system unconscious. In certain cases of schizophrenia Freud observed that the "thing presentation" in the unconscious is "lost," whilst the word representation of the object denoted is retained. That is to say, Freud observed that the relationship to human objects in certain instances was lost and that the words denoting the objects were taken by the patient as substitutes for the objects themselves.[3] As these concepts are very difficult to follow, the editors of Freud's *Standard Works* noted that Freud defined the concept of object representation in an early neurological work on aphasia as follows, and I quote from this work (Freud, 1891):

> The word, then, is a complicated concept built up from various impressions, i.e., it corresponds to an intricate process of associations entered into by elements of visual, acoustic and kinesthetic origins. However, the word acquires its significance through its association with the 'idea' (concept) of the object, at least if we restrict our consideration to nouns. The idea, or concept, of the object is itself another complex of associations composed of the most varied visual, auditory, tactile, kinesthetic, and other impressions. According to the philosophical teaching, the idea of the object contains nothing else; the appearance of a 'thing,' the 'properties' of which are conveyed to us by our senses, originates only from the fact that in enumerating the sensory impressions received from an object we allow for the possibility of a large series of new impressions being added to the chain of associations (John Stuart Mill) [p. 77].[4]

Freud was acquainted with the works of John Stuart Mill, as he had been his German translator. Mill was the last great British empiricist and representational psychologist. Freud here uncritically accepts Locke's concept of the object representation as an "atomic" thing in itself that in some measure corresponds to the physical object that had induced it in the mind.

Perhaps we still require the term object representation if only to remind ourselves that we are referring to a psychological object and not the object in physical space. However,

3 See Chapter VII for a further discussion of this point.
4 Freud here refers to John Stuart Mill's work on logic.

it carries with it the unfortunate connotation of representational psychology, that the subject is simply a passive receptacle of emanations arising from the object in physical space—that the object representation "in the mind" is a simple entity. The concept of object representation is now well entrenched within psychoanalytic theory. For example, recently an eminent psychoanalytic clinician, Jacobson, made much use of the concept of "self and object representations." Although she does not conceive the mind to be a passive instrument, nor does she believe in any simple atomistic concept of the self and the object, the use of such terms does perpetuate an image derived from representational psychology. Jacobson gives the terms "self" and "object" representation a central place in her theory of object relations (Jacobson, 1964). Whether this was intended or not, it perpetuates the notion that there are discrete and separate structures in the mind corresponding to the discrete atomistic entities of representational psychology (for a discussion of a psychoanalytic theory of the "self" representation, see Chapter IX).

Hume and the "Reality System"

Once the distinction between subject and object was accepted, as it was in pre-Platonic Greek thought, one had to account for the distinction between inner and outer reality, that is, between imagination and perception. It would seem that all of the great philosophers considered this problem, and the reader will not be burdened with a review of their thinking. We shall, however, examine Hume's explanation, for again in some small measure his notions may have influenced Freud's thinking. For Hume, the distinction between ideas that are the result of perception and considered to be real and ideas that are merely imagined was based upon a quantitative factor—that is, the intensity or vivacity of the idea. "An idea of the imagination may acquire such a force and

vivacity as to pass for an idea of the memory, and counter-
feit its effects on the belief and judgment" (Hume, *A Treatise
of Human Nature,* p. 79). Hume also noted: "An idea of the
memory, by losing its force and vivacity, may degenerate to
such a degree, as to be taken for an idea of the imagination"
(p. 78).

In *The Ego and the Id* (1930, p. 23), Freud refers to a
similar quantitative explanation. He speaks of the intensity
of ideas as a hypercathexis which may lead to the acceptance
of some ideas as "real." "When a hypercathexis of the process
of thinking takes place, thoughts are *actually* perceived—as
if they come from without—and are consequently held to be
true."

Hume also speaks of a *system* of the mind concerned with
reality. Such ideas of mental systems concerned with the function of testing reality may have anticipated the psychoanalytic
concepts of the ego as an organized system of functions. We
do not know whether or not Freud was acquainted with these
ideas of Hume's, but it is likely that similar notions formed
some part of his early education. We quote now from Hume,
A Treatise of Human Nature (p. 99):

> It is evident that whatever is present to the memory, striking
> upon the mind with a vivacity which resembles an immediate
> impression, must become of considerable moment in all the
> operations of the mind, and must easily distinguish itself
> above the mere fictions of the imagination. Of these impres-
> sions or ideas of the memory we form a kind of system, com-
> prehending whatever we remember to have been present,
> either to our internal perception or senses; and every par-
> ticular of that system, joined to the present impressions, we
> are pleased to call a reality.

Although Hume speaks of a psychological system, his concept of a psychological system is quite different from the psychoanalytic concept of psychological structure. For Hume,

unlike psychoanalysis, still conceived of the mind as a passive instrument.

Kant was the first major philosopher to appreciate that the mind is not merely a passive organ for the reception of emanations from the objects of the physical world but in its turn actively structures the perception of physical objects.

Kant and the Structure of Mind

We do not know to what extent Freud was influenced by Kantian philosophy. As a cultured European he had more than a passing acquaintance with Kant's works and in several instances demonstrated this knowledge by direct quotation. (In the paper, *The Unconscious* [Freud, 1915b] and the paper entitled *The Economic Problem of Masochism* [Freud, 1924b, p. 167], Freud equates his concept of the superego with Kant's categorical imperative.)

Kant asserted in a revolutionary fashion that objective reality, to be known to all, must conform to the essential structure of the human mind (Greene, 1929). Kant conceived of the mind as an active instrument, and, unlike his predecessors, he *accepted the mind's limitations.* The previously held assumption that all reality could be known through reason (guaranteed by an omnipotent deity) was a thinly veiled belief in the omnipotence of thought. To share God's omnipotence is in fact to possess omnipotence. Kant believed that an inherent structure of mind (we would today say a biological structure) limits the sectors of reality that can be apprehended. Kant believed, as did Descartes, but not Locke, in the existence of innate or *a priori* ideas. He stated: "But although all our knowledge begins with experience, it does not follow that it arises from experience" (Kant, *Introduction to Critique of Pure Reason*). Belief in innate ideas may seem old-fashioned to some contemporary psychologists, but psychoanalytic observation as well as the observations of ethologists (Lorenz, 1963) indicate that there is genetically transmitted information concerning an environment that the individual has not yet experienced. Anna Freud states (1951) that on the basis of direct child observation there exists in the child innate preformed attitudes that are not originated but are merely stimulated by life experiences. She observed, for example, that young children who were not raised by their parents, that is, who were transferred from a hospital to a nursery at the age of 10 days, and who had no possible opportunity for observing adults in the act of intercourse, would play at imitating coitus.

The acceptance of the distinction between the subject and the object (within the individual and the culture) is only gradually and painfully acquired. It is only with the greatest reluctance that man accepts the fact of an inanimate "nature" that cannot be influenced by his wishes. With the gradual relinquishing of one's belief in one's own omnipotence there is persistent belief that omnipotent powers do exist and that under suitable conditions God's omnipotence or that of his agents, the priests, can be shared by the individual. It is to Kant's everlasting achievement that he brought this belief to its final end. Kant continued to believe in God but he did not believe that God shared his omnipotence with men.

Kant's distinction between inner subjective experience and outer reality is based upon an acceptance of man's limitations. For Kant the crucial difference between subjective and objective experience is the ability to *control* or *determine* the spatial or temporal pattern of what is sensuously perceived (Greene, 1929). One can control the subjective wish but cannot control that which is outside of the self.

An object of experience then is that which is endowed with a spatial and temporal order which cannot be altered by an act of will. That is, when one perceives a moving ship or chair one cannot alter the perception. One, however, can imagine a chair in any fashion that one wishes [Quoted by Greene, 1929].

Freud reasoned along similar lines. However, he reversed the illustration. For Kant, sensory experience, such as the image of a moving ship, was that which could not be controlled by the imagination. For Freud it was the inner environment, the demands of instinct, that could not be simply deflected by a wish. He described the infant's capacity to differentiate an outside from an inside in the following terms:

> Let us imagine ourselves in the situation of an almost entirely helpless living organism, as yet unoriented in the world, which is receiving stimuli in its nervous substance. This organism will very soon be in a position to make a first distinction and a first orientation. On the one hand, it will be aware of stimuli which can be avoided by muscular action (flight); these it ascribes to an external world. On the other hand, it will also be aware of stimuli against which such action is of no avail and whose character of constant pressure persists in spite of it; these stimuli are the signs of an internal world, the evidence of instinctual needs. The perceptual substance of the living organism will thus have found in the efficacy of his muscular activity a basis for distinguishing between an 'outside' and 'inside' [Freud, 1915a, p. 119].

The Many Realities

Psychoanalysis accepts both a social and relativistic interpretation of reality. Social in the sense that the attribute "real" refers to the sharing of inferences regarding the external world. This view was anticipated by William James, who referred to the reali*ties*, to subuniverses of reality. There is, he stated, the reality of the senses, which is the ordinary world of physical objects; there is a subuniverse of science, as well as the world of what he called "idols of the tribe"— the sharing of myths and illusions (James, 1890).

The physicist Eddington compared the reality of common sense experience with the world of science, employing his famous simile of two tables. His first table is the familiar, substantial table of the everyday world. His second table is a scientific table (Eddington, 1928):

> My scientific table is mostly emptiness. Sparsely scattered in that emptiness are numerous electrical charges rushing about with great speed; but the combined bulk amounts to less than a billionth of the bulk of the table itself.

We cannot say that Eddington's first table is "realer" than his second. James would say that the two tables belonged to different subuniverses of reality; they represent different ways of structuring reality.

In our first chapter we referred to Kuhn's work concerning the history of science. He would say that reality is structured by the scientists in accordance with a shared schemata or paradigm. According to Kuhn, science does not discover "truer" realities but simply changes its paradigms so that observations may fit more adequately. With each scientific revolution, nature is seen in a different way. Kuhn emphasizes the implicit discontinuity that occurs when a new paradigm is adopted; there is a radical revision of the view of the world. A similar point of view was expressed in an entirely different field—that of the history of art. Gombrich (1960) explodes the notion that there was a time in the history of art when painters simply copied nature. This tradition was based on a belief in absolute reality, a reality which the artist is skilled enough to duplicate. Gombrich shows that this is not true for art—for what is accepted as "nature" is determined by stylistic convention.

Nature is not copied but it is sorted out or interpreted in accordance with certain shared or traditional schemata. This view of reality has also been expressed by Whorf (1956), who considers that the structure of language serves as a rigid schema that determines how "reality" is interpreted. All of these views share to some extent an essentially Kantian belief: that the activity of mind structures the nature of "reality." I have also indicated throughout this work my indebtedness to Cassirer who is perhaps the foremost contemporary Kantian.

We may, for ease of comprehension, divide these many spheres of reality into four related sets or classes: the public, and the private; and the autonomous, that is, the relatively unmodifiable, as opposed to the more plastic. As members of the same species we share certain genetic information concerning the environment, but the poet Blake has written that "the fool sees not the same tree that a wise man sees." There is, as this poet apprehended, a vision of the world that is private and idiosyncratic as opposed to what is public and shared.

Although there are individual differences in the development of autonomous perceptual apparatuses, in most instances the differences are not significant. An exception would be in those cases where the ego apparatus is itself atrophied or failed to develop because of an actual absence of maternal care, such as Spitz (1945) has described in certain cases of infants in institutions.

Our genetic inheritance fixes certain limits to the ego apparatuses: a selective capacity to respond to certain stimuli from the environment and to exclude others. This is analogous to the theory proposed by Von Uexküll (1934) that each species responds to limited sectors of the environment. So there is an aspect of the capacity of the mind to apprehend reality that is fixed and limited by biology. It would be a mistake, however, to contrast the biological with the cultural, for our phylogenetic inheritance also provides for the capacity to create culture. We noted earlier that the cave art of Cro-Magnon man that was unknown to his less intelligent

Neanderthal predecessor may reflect in part a genetic mutation, a mutation that permits the creation and the apprehension of symbolic thought. Modern linguistic research (Chomsky, 1965) leads to a similar conclusion, for the capacity to assign meaning to sentences is a function of such complexity that the child who is learning to speak cannot possibly have learned to assign meaning to sounds entirely from experience. We are forced to assume that the individual child has genetically transmitted information that enables him to assign meaning to the sequence of sounds that we call human speech, that is to say, that the task is of such enormous complexity that it cannot have been learned piecemeal. Sentences possess an innate structure—the capacity to apprehend this structure, that is, to assign meaning, is probably genetically determined. The content of the language must, of course, be learned. As Chomsky indicates, modern linguistic research confirms Descartes' belief in innate ideas. So that in a certain sense language provides a public and shared structuring of reality as opposed to a privately structured reality.

However, in another sense, as Blake testified, the structuring of reality remains private. As we hope to show in the next chapter, the structures of the mind that determine the individual's relation to reality and his capacity to test reality —his capacity to disinguish beween wish and perception— are inextricably bound to both the quality of his earliest human love relationships and to the gratification that is afforded him by human beings in the present. *The capacity to know and the capacity to love are not, as older facultative psychology would suggest, entirely separate functions.*[5]

---

[5] An exception to this statement would be the observation that some people who have impaired capacities to love have contributed to the sum total of human knowledge. Psychoanalytic observation of certain of these creative people suggests that they have an impaired capacity to know in the sense of learning from others. Their knowledge tends to be self-created in a manner analogous to the self-creation of their environment (See Chapter III).

Chapter VI

OBJECT LOVE AND THE STRUCTURING OF REALITY

As we have described in the previous chapter, the organization of reality is in part a social phenomenon and, as such, cannot be separated from those structures of the mind that determine man's relation to other human beings. If one is not able to identify with other people, or indeed acknowledge the existence of others, one cannot partake in the social structuring of reality. We wish here to bring our earlier description of the maturation of object love into accord with what may seem to be a separate function but is at bottom inextricably connected—the development of the capacity to accept painful reality.

Certain comparisons between animal and human development may help to bring these very complex issues into sharper focus, and I shall review some observations that have been presented earlier.

The modern science of ethology has convincingly demonstrated that information concerning a yet-unexperienced environment is transmitted genetically. The development of the capacity to sort out or structure the environment in accordance with the survival needs of the organism is analogous to the development of the bodily organs. Such behavioral structures have indeed been labeled organs (without quotation marks) by Lorenz (1963). In many species, especially social animals, the normal development of a given behavioral organ is contingent upon the actions of other members of the same species. There are certain required responses from other individuals of the species, required at a certain strictly specified point in time in order for the behavioral organ to develop normally.

There are probably some vestiges in man of these analogous, genetically determined "behavioral organs" which also require the "fitting in" of other human beings at crucial points in time.[1] For example, Spitz observed that hospitalized infants who were properly fed and received hygienic care, but were deprived of mothering, suffered severe retardation of ego development. His observations have been confirmed by other careful studies (Provence and Lipton, 1962; Provence and Ritvo, 1961).

These and similar observations can be placed within the context of Hartmann's concept of autonomous ego development. We no longer believe, as Freud did, that the ego is formed in its entirety as a result of conflict between the instincts and the environment. There are some ego functions whose analogue can be found in lower animals, functions vouchsafed by inheritance, whose development is relatively uninfluenced by conflict. Deterioration or atrophy of these autonomous structures occurs only in the most extreme conditions, such as the near total absence of protective human beings in early infancy. For those children who have been subjected to massive neglect of this sort, the outcome is likely to be a form of childhood schizophrenia. In most cases of adult schizophrenia and in the borderline group, there is no evidence of such a massive neglect in the early years of life. What can be reconstructed from the history of adult schizophrenic and borderline patients is not the *absence* of a ma-

---

[1] The integration of the findings of ethology within the body of psychoanalytic knowledge has been the subject of a recent symposium (Tidd, Bowlby, and Kaufman, 1960).

ternal environment but a relative *failure* of the maternal environment. There is, I believe, relatively normal development of the so-called autonomous ego functions in these
people.

The structuring of reality by the autonomous development of the perceptual apparatus is more or less uniform.
Individual differences do, of course, exist with regard to any
bodily characteristic, but the differences are not significant.
The human child, however, depends upon his protective parents for knowledge of the dangers of the environment to a
greater extent than any other animal species. The greatest
danger to the human child is separation from the parents.
However, the child fears not only the actual physical separation from the parents but also the instinctual (not instinctive)
demands he places upon the parents—demands which en-
danger his relationship to them will also result in anxiety.[2]

There is a highly complex, twofold aspect to the structuring of reality which results from this prolonged dependency.
On the one hand, the child is dependent upon its parents to
provide the knowledge of the dangers of the environment
that is necessary for survival. In this sense the mother *is*
the child's earliest environment. The child depends upon the
mother to perform certain executant functions which it is
only later able to perform for itself. On the other hand, the
very conditions of excessive dependency lead to anxiety and
the creation of a private inner world. For the dread of loss
and abandonment (Rochlin, 1965) provides the motive force
for the creation of another world, a world that is more in
keeping with the child's wish—the magical world, the world

[2] Bowlby's attempt (1960) to interpret separation anxiety as strictly equivalent to an ethological mechanism ignores the difference between the more
plastic instinctual process as compared with the rigidly specified instinct of
lower animals. Separation anxiety reflects the interaction of mechanisms that
are characteristic of the human species with other automatisms that have been
inherited from lower animals. For a similar criticism, see the discussion of
Bowlby's paper by A. Freud, Schur, and Spitz, 1960).

of interconnectedness between symbol and the object symbolized. In this world, separation and death are denied, for possession of a symbol of the object guarantees the existence of the object itself. As a paradigm of the child's use of symbols in the creation of the inner world we refer the reader back to Freud's description of a child's game. There, you will remember, the child dropped and retrieved a spool over the side of its crib. By this magical gesture the child created an illusory world in which he could control his mother's going and coming.

We have discussed in earlier chapters that there may be either some interpenetration between the knowledge gained from perception and magical thought, or that the knowledge gained from perception may be disavowed. Freud referred to the child's game as a great cultural achievement, in that it permitted an instinctual renunciation, that is, it allowed the child to permit his mother to go away. The child's magical thought performed an adaptive service.

There are other examples from pathology where the function of magical thought is less adaptive. In these instances the painful aspects of reality are completely disavowed, leading to what Freud described as a split in the ego (Freud, 1927, 1940b). I have understood such a persistent split in the ego to be the outcome of a failure in the development of those same structures that vouchsafe the capacity for mature love; this leads to a developmental arrest at the stage of transitional objects. I have proposed in Chapter IV that this developmental arrest may be the result of a failure to identify with a good parental object—a failure of the "holding environment" leads to a failure of identification. Such a failure has momentous effects. It leads to the persistence of "untamed" instinctual demands, a relative inability to tolerate frustration, an inability to tolerate the limitations of loved objects. Such an intolerance is displaced upon the world at large and is experienced as an inability to accept the pain and frustration of reality.

In patients that we have observed, it would appear that the balance of love and hate is weighted in the direction of the destructive instincts. While it is possible that such people may have been endowed at birth with a quantitatively greater degree of destructive instinct, making the task of accepting restraints of civilization more difficult, this is unproven. What can be reconstructed from observation is that there has been, in all instances, a relative failure of the maternal environment.

Let us now attempt to summarize our concepts in a somewhat schematic fashion: I have found support in the observation of borderline and schizophrenic people for Hartmann's suggestion that there is a twofold aspect of the ego's structuring of reality. To adopt the language of ethology, there are at least two organs for the structuring of reality. One consists of those autonomous ego structures that are genetically determined—the perceptual apparatuses that permit the distinction between self and object in physical space; in these instances individual differences in perception are not significant, as the development of the perceptual apparatuses is relatively independent of individual life experience. These apparatuses require the presence of an object for their development, but except in extreme instances we believe that there is relatively normal development of these autonomous ego apparatuses in adult schizophrenic and borderline patients. The second organ for the organization of reality is that with which we are most concerned. This is a structure that is not vouchsafed by inheritance but must be formed anew in each individual. It is, as we have observed, a structure that requires for its healthy development (to use Winnicott's term) "good enough mothering." *Autonomous structures will be impaired if there is an absence of the maternal environment; this more plastic organ for the structuring of reality will be impaired if there is a failure of the maternal environment.*

Freud acknowledged the capacity to accept painful reality to be the essential issue in the ego's relationship to reality (Freud, 1911a).[3] At bottom, the content of human suffering is fairly uniform; separation and loss of loved objects—the idea of death and castration (in the male) is added later as a mental content (Freud, 1926). The problem of the acceptance of painful reality can then be reduced to the problem of accepting the separateness of objects—that they can be lost. For, as we have noted in our earlier discussion of omnipotent thought, the fundamental aim of magical thinking is to create the illusion that the symbol and the object symbolized are inseparable. The magical world is a world in which nothing is lost, in which there are no limits to time or space—separation, death, and castration are negated.

It is the central theme of this monograph that *the acceptance of painful reality rests upon the same ego structures that permit the acceptance of the separateness of objects.* To state it in the obverse: the ego structure whose development permits the acceptance of painful reality is identical to that psychic structure whose development enables one to love maturely. In both instances the signposts that indicate whether or not such a successful historical development has been traversed is the sense of identity. If one is fortunate enough to have received "good enough mothering" in the first and second years of life, the core of a positive sense of identity will have been formed. This core permits the partial relinquishment of instinctual demands upon the object and in turn permits the partial acceptance of the separateness of objects. It is this process upon which reality testing hinges.

---

[3] A new principle of mental functioning was thus introduced; what was presented in the mind was no longer what was agreeable but what was real, even if it happened to be disagreeable. The setting up of the *reality principle* proved to be a momentous step (Freud, 1911a, p. 219).

Freud (1911a), in his paper, *Formulations on the Two Principles of Mental Functioning,* attributed to the development of the reality principle the capacity to postpone the need for direct gratification, that is, to postpone direct motor action. He linked the development of this capacity to the development of the process of thinking, which he described as "an experimental kind of acting":

> Restraint upon motor discharge (upon action), which then became necessary, was provided by means of the process of thinking, which was developed from the presentation of ideas. Thinking was endowed with characteristics which made it possible for the mental apparatus to tolerate an increased tension of stimulus while the process of discharge was postponed. It is essentially an experimental kind of acting, accompanied by displacement of relatively small quantities of cathexis together with less expenditure (discharge) of them. For this purpose the conversion of freely displaceable cathexis into 'bound' cathexis was necessary, and this was brought about by means of raising the level of the whole cathectic process [p. 221].

In this fundamental paper Freud did not attribute this process to the maturation of object relations. However, there is an implicit connection in that he suggests that the persistence of magical thinking is related to the persistence of autoeroticism. (We shall return to this examination of Freud's views later in this chapter.)

The Difference between the Body Schema and the Body Image

The distinction between an autonomous and a more plastic ego structure may be further illustrated by comparing the body schema and the body image. The English neurologist, Lord Brain, has suggested that the perception of the externality of objects is inferred by means of a body schema (Brain, 1951):

In our awareness of our bodies we are directly aware of a three-dimensional object. The position of this object can be changed in relation to the external world, and the position of its parts can be modified in relation to the body as a whole. Thus, the body serves as a primary model of three-dimensional space [p. 17].

The body schema can be compared with a different concept—the body image. This is an organization, partly unconscious, of one's earliest memories and fantasies concerning the body—especially the face and genitals. In contrast to the body schema it is a highly individualized, idiosyncratic structure. It forms, as Freud and others have noted (Greenacre, 1958), the earliest outlines of the sense of identity. The body schema is a relatively standardized biological given; the body image is the outcome of individual historical process. The body schema enables one to make correct inferences regarding the position of other objects in physical space; the body image enables inferences to be made concerning people in "social" space.

Reality Testing

The problem of reality testing, the capacity to distinguish between the fantasies, images, and hallucinations of the inner world and the perceptions of the external world, is, as we noted in Chapter V, an ancient one. The functions involved are so complex that most psychoanalytic observers break down the concept into separate parts. Weisman (1965), for example, distinguishes the sense of reality (that is, the conviction that something is real) from the testing of reality. Frosch (1964) distinguishes the relationship to reality from the testing of reality. When several authors attempt to establish different categories of thought, it is not surprising that there is not uniform agreement regarding the use of these terms. While I do not find myself in complete agreement

with either author regarding definitions, I have been com-
pelled by clinical observation to follow Frosch's distinction
between the testing of reality and the relationship to reality.
This is not simply an arbitrary distinction, for this distinction
also corresponds to certain rough nosological categories. The
borderline character and certain schizophrenic people suffer
from disturbances in reality testing, but as we shall describe,
they maintain an interest in others and in the world in general. They may hate reality, but they do not lose interest
in it.[4]

There is another group of patients who have a different
relationship to reality—they have, in fact, abandoned interest (to a greater or lesser degree) in people and have turned
instead to find a substitute for reality, a source of gratification in themselves—in their own bodies and in their mental
processes. I have observed that hallucinations are the principal means by which this substitute gratification is achieved
(Modell, 1958, 1960). Auditory hallucinations serve as substitutes for people—they are experienced by the patient as
friends, advisors, sexual partners, as well as the more commonly recognized role of harsh critics. Some schizophrenic
patients develop hallucinations whilst others do not. We do
not know why this is true, but it is a fact that in those cases
where hallucinations develop there is a fundamental alteration in the individual's relation to reality. For this reason I
shall discuss this process separately in the next chapter.

In borderline and schizophrenic patients the autonomous
organs for the perception of reality remain intact, while
the failure of identification leads to a failure to accept the
separateness of objects. This means that such people can

---

4 Frosch does not agree with this account, for he believes that the relationship to reality is disturbed in borderline and psychotic characters, whereas
reality testing remains intact. I do not know whether this represents a fundamental disagreement regarding the data of observation or whether it simply
represents a failure to agree on nosological categories.

and do form a "correct" judgment of the external world, but this judgment is disavowed and denied. Freud (1940a) stated in his *Outline of Psychoanalysis:*

> The problem of psychosis would be simple and perspicuous if the ego's detachment from reality could be carried through completely. But that seems to happen only rarely or perhaps never. But even in the state so far removed from the reality of the external world as one of hallucinatory confusion, one learns from patients after their recovery that at the time, in some corner of their mind (as they put it) there was a normal person hidden who, like a detached spectator, watched the hubbub of illness go past him [p. 201].

The distortion of perceptual knowledge in psychosis usually refers to a distortion of the perception of a feeling state in other people. The well-known mechanism of projection is one in which an inner feeling state, one of hatred, is attributed to an external object. We know that the recognition of affect in members of the same and other species is a phylogenetically ancient acquisition. The ability to assess correctly an emotional state is of the greatest adaptive significance; a misinterpretation of a feeling state amongst animals could be fatal. The capacity to respond to and recognize the mood of others is believed to be, at least by one eminent biologist, Portmann (1961), present in even the lowly insect.

Anyone who has owned a dog knows that dogs are exquisitely attuned to the affects of other dogs and are also quite sensitive to changes in the mood of their masters. Human infants and young children also demonstrate this primitive capacity to assess correctly the emotional state of their mothers. We referred previously to Anna Freud's observation that children in wartime did not respond with fear to bombs falling about them but responded only to their mothers' anxiety. From the standpoint of the biology of behavior it would seem highly improbable that such a vital and ancient function should be "lost" in schizophrenic and borderline individuals.

There is more direct evidence that this is not the case. Those who have attempted to treat psychotic people discover that although one portion of their minds uncritically accepts a reality that is fashioned in accordance with the needs of their inner world, with another portion of their minds they are shrewd and excellent observers. Searles (1965), a psychoanalyst who has devoted his professional life to the psychotherapeutic treatment of schizophrenia, reports that his patients have confronted him with accurate appraisals of aspects of his character of which he had previously been only partially aware.

The problem of reality testing is at bottom the problem of denial—the need to disavow painful perceptions and to substitute a view of the world that is more in keeping with omnipotent wishes. I have suggested that this function is regulated by the same ego structure that permits the formation of more mature object relationships. In both instances, in the acceptance of reality and the acceptance of a loved person, that which is painful must be acknowledged.

We have also described the fact that the wish to merge, to fuse with the loved object, to lose one's identity, cannot in itself be labeled pathological. On the one hand, we can describe an arrest in the development of a sense of identity that underlies the failure of reality testing in borderline and schizophrenic patients; but on the other, we may consider that in the so-called normal individual, whose sense of identity has matured adequately, there may be a wish to undo what has been achieved. That is to say, we have to consider normal regression as well as pathological failure of development. In both instances there may be a loss of reality testing. In an individual who has a capacity for mature love, such loss of reality testing may be transitory and in a sense controlled, whereas in others who have actually suffered a structural arrest, loss of reality testing may be more lasting and not subject to control. Reality testing, then, is highly complex. It is not, as some authors suggest, an ego function that works on the all-or-none principle. At certain times everyone may experience some confusion regarding that which belongs to the self and that which arises from the external world.

Case Illustration[5]

The following observations were obtained in the course of psychotherapeutic work with a woman who had been hospitalized for several years and who improved enough to return home. Her diagnosis was that of a paranoid schizophrenic, and her central delusion concerned her relationship to her husband. She would observe used tissues in her pocketbook or on various surfaces of her house. Usually these scraps of tissue would be ignored. However, at certain times their discovery would precipitate an intense outburst of rage against her husband. She would accuse him of having used these tissues for masturbation and purposely confronting her with this "evidence" in order to drive her crazy.

After a considerable period of psychotherapeutic work, the meaning of this delusion was clarified. The accusation directed against her husband was intended for her mother, for she believed that he was throwing away a precious body substance that she desired. He was willfully wasting his semen, as her mother had, she believed, willfully wasted the contents of her breasts on other children. In this delusional formation semen was symbolically equated with milk.

During these delusional periods she lost all sense of identity. Her ego became fragmented, and the various identifications that formerly comprised her poorly integrated and evanescent sense of self were attributed to others in a kaleido-

[5] I am indebted to Dr. Robert Farkas, who permitted me to report this case whose treatment I supervised.

scope fashion. She perceived objects as physically separate, that is, she had no question that she was talking to a man she called her husband; yet psychologically he was not her husband—he was her mother. The rage she felt toward her mother was reexperienced without any mitigation or possibility of modification.

With the complete dissolution of the sense of self, she was unable to conceive of the existence of other objects as separate from the self. That is to say, the true identity of objects in her environment was no longer accepted; in turn, she clothed them with an identity that arose from within. Her husband had ceased to exist as a separate object, as she had ceased to exist as a distinct individual.

With the failure to distinguish self and objects we find a complete dissolution of the distinction between inner and outer worlds. We do not know whether the mother had actually frustrated her in infancy in the manner that she claimed. However, the belief in a frustrating mother, who throws the contents of her breasts on the floor in order to taunt, was an unquestioned part of her inner reality. The dramatis personae of her inner world were a totally frustrating mother and a helpless, starving child. This pitiable drama would be reenacted toward other persons in her environment in total disregard of the actual identity of the objects. For example, her three-year-old child would at times also be involved in this delusional formation. As she had clothed her husband in her mother's costume, so she identified her three-year-old child as her own deprived infantile self. At these times she, the patient, would be cast in the role of the frustrating mother and then would actually refuse to feed her child. Objects of the external world are invested with the qualities of objects in the inner world; actual perceptions are denied.

Though the quality of objects in this patient's world corresponded to an inner rather than an external reality, she did

not lose interest in these people. Although she would rage
against her husband and would frustrate her child and mis-
identify them in the manner we have described, she remained
interested in them. This is in contrast to hallucinating patients whose hallucinations, objects of the inner world, become substitutes for objects of the actual world.

Reality and Group Identity

In Chapter V we concluded that reality consists of sharing
a conventional schema that serves to organize the perception
of the external world; reality is defined in a social sense. How
then can individuals share conventional schemata if each person experiences the world idiosyncratically? If we agree with
Blake that the fool sees not the same tree that a wise man
sees, that each one of us experiences the world uniquely, how
can knowledge of the environment be shared? We do not intend to enter the field of linguistics or epistomology but wish
to point to a purely psychological answer to this question
that is implicit in Freud's (1921) monograph on *Group Psychology*. Freud believed that the existence of human groups
depends upon some form of object love. Group members dif-
fer from lovers in that the gratifications achieved were not the
direct, instinctual gratifications of lovers. As is true of individual love relationships, group ties depend upon the process
of identification.

> What we learned from these three sources may be summa-
> rized as follows. First, identification is the original form of
> emotional tie with an object; secondly, in a regressive way it
> becomes a substitute for a libidinal object-tie, as it were, by
> means of introjection of the object into the ego; and thirdly,
> it may rise with any new perception of a common quality
> shared with some other person who is not an object of the
> sexual instinct. The more important this common quality is,

the more successful may this partial identification become, and it may thus represent the beginning of a new tie [p. 107].

In this essay Freud described a group formation as a sharing of a common ideal, that is, an identification with the leader:

> A primary group of this kind is a number of individuals who have put one and the same object in the place of their ego ideal and have consequently identified themselves with one another in their ego [p. 116].

By means of identification they, therefore, share a similar psychic structure, a similar ego ideal. That is, a piece of the external world has been collectively incorporated. Freud noted that groups with leaders are a special instance, for he also recognized that identification may arise "with any new perception of a common quality shared with some person who is not an object of the sexual instinct." This conception has been elaborated by Erikson (1959) to include not only an identification with a leader but an identification that results from the sharing of a common tradition of thought. This does not, of course, exclude the more specific identification with a historical or mythical leader, but identification with the hero is not the exclusive condition upon which groups are formed. In modern society identifications are multiple and overlapping. One may identify with a national group, ethnic class, religious group, professional group, etc. Identification in each instance implies the assimilation of a commonly held tradition or schema. By means of group identification we are able to share a similar structuring of the environment so that a group identification is in essence a structuring of reality. We are now able to understand the process that underlies William James' "many subuniverses of reality." His world of senses or physical things would correspond to the autonomous

ego function of perceiving objects in space. The world of
reality of science, the world of ideal relations or abstract
truths, and the world of what James called "idols of the
tribe" would correspond to a variety of group identifications
—commonly held schemata that serve to organize the uni-
verse. In the same essay James (1890) refers to the following
passage from Josiah Royce who saw man's need to impose the
regularity of structure:

> Put a man into a perfect chaos of phenomena—sounds,
> sights, feelings—and if the man continued to exist, and to be
> rational at all, his attention would doubtless soon find for
> him a way to make some kind of rhymic regularity, which
> he would impute to the things about him, so as to imagine
> that he had discovered some law of sequence in this mad new
> world. And thus, in every case where we fancy ourselves sure
> of a simple law of nature, we must remember that a great
> deal of the fancied simplicity may be due, in a given case,
> not to nature but to the inerradicable prejudice of our
> minds in favor of regularity and simplicity [p. 316].

Erikson (1959) has observed the transitional processes between individual idiosyncratic identifications formed within
the family and the expanding identifications with a variety of
social groups. As our group ties overlap and are numerous,
we share many overlapping and at times contradictory schemata of reality. An amusing illustration was provided by
Keynes (1956) in a charming biographical note concerning
Newton. After having examined a voluminous quantity of
Newton's manuscripts, Keynes concluded that during the
very years that he, Newton, was composing his "Principia,"
he was an unbridled addict of magic and alchemy. He kept
this interest secret, and the evidence of these magical investigations was conveniently ignored by earlier biographers who
wished to preserve the myth of a completely rational Newton.
Yet Keynes asserts that there are at least ten thousand words

in these manuscripts that are entirely concerned with magic and devoid of any scientific value.

We recall that Freud (1921) described the primitive origin of identification as the oral wish to devour. Identification results in part in a magical illusion, that is, the illusion of acquiring the quality of the object itself by means of the possession of the symbol, or part of the object. Freud refers, for example, to the cannibal who believes that by eating a part of the enemy he acquires his enemy's strength. Although identification leads to an illusion that minimizes the differences between the subject and the object, it is an illusion without which we cannot live; it is the basis of group ties.

Erikson (1965) and Greenson (1953) have shown that the process of identification may also work in the negative. That is, we may wish to avoid similarity between ourselves and others by perceiving *only* the differences, that is, we may wish to avoid identification. Although we are all one species, by a selective denial of similarities, we may place certain individuals outside of our group and thus be able to hate or destroy those who are felt to be alien. Erikson refers in his essay to the attitude of American whites toward the Negro. Group ties, therefore, perform the essential function of creating the illusion of the sharing of an identical schema of the external world.

Freud's Concept of the Reality Principle

We have tried to show that our capacity to accept painful reality is molded by the same psychic structures and early experiences that determine our capacity to accept the frustration inherent in human relationships. Learning and loving are in this sense highly interrelated. The capacity to truly identify, not merely to imitate, parallels the capacity to really "take something in," and not merely to parrot knowledge. Our observation that the development of object relations cannot be separated from the development of the reality functions of the ego is by no means original; the connection between these two processes was recognized by Ferenczi as early as 1913. (See also Hartmann, 1956). But this observation is not in accord with the "common sense" assumption of the older facultative psychology that would place cognition and feeling in separate compartments of the mind. In Freud's own contribution the connection between object love and reality functions remains implicit rather than explicit.

In Freud's earliest and most fundamental contribution— *The Two Principles of Mental Functioning* (1911), the development of the reality principle is linked to the ego's function of self-preservation:

> Just as the pleasure principle can do nothing but *wish*, work for the yield of pleasure, avoid unpleasure, so the reality-ego need do nothing but strive for what is *useful* and guard itself against damage [p. 233].

Freud's explication of the process of denial and the splitting of the ego (which form the foundation of this chapter) was presented in a later series of papers extending from the middle 1920s until his death. The list includes: *The Loss of Reality in Neurosis and Psychosis* (1924a); *Negation* (1925); *Fetishism* (1927); the unfinished manuscript, *The Splitting of the Ego in the Process of Defense* (1940b); and finally, *An Outline of Psychoanalysis* (1940a), which was written shortly before his death. In *Negation,* not only was reality testing attributed to the ability to differentiate internal from external, but, for the first time, note was taken of the significance of early object relations in the development of this ego function:

> The antithesis between subjective and objective does not exist from the first. It only comes into being from the fact that thinking possesses the capacity to bring before the mind once more something that has been perceived, by reproduc-

ing it as a presentation without the external object having still to be there. The first and immediate aim, therefore, of reality testing is, not to *find* an object in real perception which corresponds to the one presented, but to *re-find* such an object, to convince oneself that it is still there [p. 237].

But it is evident that a precondition for the setting up of reality-testing is that objects shall have been lost which once brought real satisfaction [p. 238].

In this single sentence, Freud condenses what we have been attempting to convey in this chapter. The crucial phrase is his reference to objects that "once brought real satisfaction." Objects that brought real satisfaction are "good objects," objects with which one can identify. We could paraphrase Freud's sentence by means of our reiterated statement that the capacity to identify with a "good object" is the precondition for the establishment of reality testing.

In this series of papers Freud also developed a quantitative concept. Reality testing was formulated not as an absolute all-or-none process, but one involving portions of the ego. For example, in his analysis of fetishism, he observed that a portion of the mind accepted the fact of castration and had accurate knowledge of the anatomy of the female genitalia, whilst in such individuals, in another portion of the mind, an illusion was maintained that females actually possessed a penis. Freud suggested that there is a quantitative aspect to the process of denial that differentiates neurosis from psychosis. I quote from *An Outline of Psychoanalysis* (Freud, 1940a):

We may probably take it as being generally true that what occurs in all these cases is a psychical split. Two psychical attitudes have been formed instead of a single one—one, the normal one, which takes account of reality, and another which under the influence of the instincts detaches the ego

from reality. The two exist alongside of each other. The
issue depends on their relative strength. If the second is or
becomes the stronger, the necessary precondition for psychosis is present. If the relation is reversed, then there is an
apparent cure of the delusional disorder. Actually it has only
retreated into the unconscious—just as numerous observations lead us to believe that the delusion existed ready made
for a long time before its manifest irruption [p. 202].

The split in the ego that Freud described, I suggest, corresponds to our account of "the two organs" of reality testing.

In order to accept the separateness of an external object,
something of the external world must have been brought into
the ego, that is, an identification must have occurred with
protective, loving, parental objects. The degree to which this
type of identification has been achieved must vary quantitatively. It is not an all-or-none process but something that
takes place over a period of time; the degree to which this
process has been achieved may account for the quantitative
factor in denial.

Chapter VII

THE EGO'S RELATION TO THE EXTERNAL WORLD

A Janus-faced Organization within the Ego

In Chapter IV, I referred to Nunberg's metaphorical description of transference as Janus-faced, as a process which attempts to both seek gratification in the present from the person of the analyst (the ego that faces outwards) whilst it alternately withdraws to reanimate the images of the past (the ego that faces inwards). There is, I believe, in this description, a recognition of a fundamental aspect of the organization of the ego, an aspect that has been implicit in psychoanalytic theory (Freud, *On Narcissism,* 1914), but one which has not been made sufficiently explicit. *There is a functional system within the ego, an orientation in accordance with the ego's attitude toward the source of gratification—whether gratification is sought from within or from the external world.*

Let us consider another analogy (used by Freud in *Formulations on the Two Principles of Mental Functioning,* 1911a).[1] Some animals that do not receive nourishment from

[1] A neat example of a psychical system shut off from the stimuli of the external world, and able to satisfy even its nutritional requirements autistically (to use Bleuler's term), is afforded by a bird's egg with its food supply enclosed in its shell; for it, the care provided by its mother is limited to the provision of warmth. I shall not regard it as a correction, but as an amplification of the schematic picture under discussion, if it is insisted that a system living according to the pleasure principle must have devices to enable it to withdraw from the stimuli of reality (Freud, 1911a, p. 20).

their mother, that is, from the external environment, draw their nutritional needs from the yolk of an egg, which for the purposes of our illustration can be considered part of themselves. Something of the same sort is provided for the human infant by the process of autoerotism. Instinctual demands are such that the gratification provided by the environment will never suffice; the infant is insatiable but is able to make use of its own body to partially relieve this instinctual tension. The thumb can be used as a substitute for the nipple; this practice is a prototype of certain functions that the ego will later assume (Hoffer, 1949). (It has recently been observed, by means of intrauterine photography, that thumbsucking occurs even prenatally.)

A process parallel to the one that permits the infant to find gratification from its own body has been proposed in the psychic sphere. Freud suggested that the infant is able to relieve instinctual tension by means of its capacity to hallucinate an image of the organ that he seeks—that is, the breast. The existence of infantile hallucinations of this sort remains pure conjecture. Freud, however, based this conjecture upon his knowledge of the dream process, as he believed that the capacity to obtain hallucinatory gratification by means of dreaming indicated the persistence into adult life of a function that was most characteristic of infancy. Recent physiological investigations of dream states that have demonstrated the phylogenetically early origin of dreaming strongly suggest that Freud may have been right in attributing this function to man's most primitive mental organization—the infant's mind.

We now possess an objective measure that is associated with dreaming. Rapid eye movements (REM) are more often observed in dreaming than in dreamless sleep (Roffwarg et al., 1966). These studies showed that the human infant spends more of his sleep in dreaming than older children and adults. It was discovered by this method that dreaming was not limited to the human species; rapid eye movements have been observed in all the mammals who could be subjected to laboratory procedures (Snyder, 1966). Such findings suggest that the capacity to obtain instinctual discharge from within the nervous tissue itself is a fundamental part of our genetic inheritance.

In human beings at least, some aspect of this substitute gratification from within the mind is not restricted to the state of sleep. For in waking life gratification can come from within, in the absence of environmental gratification, from daydreams and fantasies; in extreme instances, as will be described, substitute gratification may be obtained by means of hallucinations.

There is a twofold aspect to the psychoanalytic model of primitive mental functioning. The hallucination is the substitute for a piece of the external world; that is, the infant can find gratification in his own psychic substance. But in another sense, the hallucination may also enable the child to postpone the demand for gratification from the environment. In this latter sense, the hallucination can be considered a primitive stage in the process of thinking—if thinking is, as Freud defined it, a preparation for action. Freud proposed in his discussion of reality principle that when images become connected to words, the mental apparatus achieves a capacity to engage in trial action, thus achieving some mitigation of the requirement for seeking immediate gratification (Freud, 1911a). The primitive capacity to find gratification through hallucinations, that is, through one's own nervous substance, becomes later modified into the process of thinking—preparation for action upon the environment. However, this older, self-gratifying organization is retained alongside of the later development of the reality ego. A nexus is established of a twofold, Janus-faced organization of the ego—one face pointing inwards towards its own psychic substance *in order to obtain gratification from the self that is denied by the envi-*

ronment and the other facing outwards in preparation for action upon the environment to wrest gratification from it. The distinction is the *function* to which the symbolic processes are put—whether gratification is sought from within or from without. (The function of symbolism will be discussed in Chapter IX.)

Language retains this twofold aspect. Words may be used as communication, that is, as a preparation for action in order to obtain gratification from external sources. Or words can be used as substitutes for external objects; in this instance they are not denotive symbols but are used as things in themselves. They may be the child's inner possession to control and play with as he wishes and are equated in the unconscious mind with other valuable inner possessions, such as feces. Freud observed such a process in schizophrenia where the word for the object can be substituted for the object itself (Freud, 1915b). Whether words are played with as things in themselves or whether they are employed denotively is determined by a *functional* consideration.

Man's lengthy dependence upon the protection of others from the dangers of the environment may be mitigated in part through the illusion obtained by magical symbolism that he can provide gratification for himself, that he can be an omnipotent object to himself. In Chapter III we described certain character types where this fantasy of omnipotent self-sufficiency becomes the central theme of the lives of some people. These are the people who appear to be withdrawn from emotional contact with others, who act as if they do not need anything from others—who can instead provide all their needs for themselves. This character type represents in part the persistence of this archaic mode of mental functioning; the inner world provides an alternative source of gratification. The relationship of the self to the environment is thus re-created in the inner world; they can be an omnipotent transitional object to themselves. A portion of the ego itself can function as if it were an external object. This symbolic re-creation of the relationship of the ego to the environment within the ego does not necessarily correspond to a re-creation of the actual relationship of the ego to people in the environment but instead may repeat the self-created transitional object. We observe that in the drama occurring within the mind, roles are easily interchangeable—the actors can be placed in the roles that are in accordance with the omnipotent wishes.[2] This will be demonstrated when we describe a schizophrenic's experience of auditory hallucinations in a later section of this chapter.

The Function of Hallucinations

Although we have described a Janus-faced organization within the ego oriented in accordance to whether gratification is achieved from within or from without, these two sources of gratification obviously are not equivalent. An infant may hallucinate the breast, but hallucinations do not provide nourishment.

There is evidence that man never outgrows his need to be in some contact with other human beings. In fact, isolation from other people is widely used as an extreme form of punishment.

Hallucinations may occur where there is a massive withdrawal from other human beings, either through environmental deprivation or as the result of a schizophrenic illness. There are very few instances where man is actually deprived of all contacts with other humans. Prisoners who are confined to a single cell at least know that there are other human beings near, and they may have the opportunity to converse with

[2] Let us reflect that the ego now enters into the relationship of an object to the ego ideal which has been developed out of it, and that all the interplay between an external object and the ego as a whole, with which our study of the neurosis has made us acquainted, may possibly be repeated upon this new scene of action within the ego (Freud, 1921, p. 130).

their jailers. However, circumstances of absolute privation, that is, complete loss of contact with others, have been described in two reports of men who sailed a long ocean voyage completely alone. One report is that of Captain Joshua Slocum, in 1890, and the other is a more recent account by Manry, an amateur sailor who sailed his tiny sloop from Falmouth, Massachusetts, to Falmouth, England (*Life*, September 17, 1965). Both solitary voyagers developed hallucinations. Slocum's (1890) description follows (he had developed intestinal cramps and went below deck to his cabin in the midst of a storm):

> How long I lay there I could not tell, for I became delirious. When I came to, as I thought, from my swoon, I realized that the sloop was plunging into a heavy sea, and looking out of the companionway, to my amazement, I saw a tall man at the helm. His rigid hand, grasping the spokes of the wheel, held them as in a vise. One can imagine my astonishment. His rig was that of a foreign sailor and the large red cap he wore was cockbilled over his left ear, and all was set off with shaggy whiskers. He would have been taken for a pirate in any part of the world. While I gazed upon his threatening aspect I forgot the storm and wondered if he had come to cut my throat. This he seemed to divine. 'Signor,' said he, doffing his hat, 'I have come to do you no harm.' And a smile, the faintest in the world, but still a smile, played on his face which seemed not unkind when he spoke. 'I have come to do you no harm—I have sailed free,' he said, 'but was never worse than a contrabandista. I am one of Columbus's crew,' he continued. 'I am the pilot of the Pinta come to aid you. Lie quiet, Signor Capitaine,' he added, 'and I will guard your ship tonight . . .' [p. 39].

Manry's hallucinations were less specific and detailed. He described in the *Life* article that he heard voices coming from the wake, calling for help. At another time he thought that he was in the place of the Sea Mountains, controlled by a man named McGregor. He stated that he sailed in circles and met a little gremlin character who said, "The trouble is that you have been sailing clockwise. You have to sail counterclockwise to get out." And this he did. In addition to the hallucinations, Manry began to develop the illusion that his little boat was a human object—he would talk to her, that is, scold her and praise her, and he began to talk of himself and the boat as "we." It is possible that his capacity to create an illusory human object relationship made further hallucinatory development unnecessary.[3]

We have described earlier two forms of human object relationships—the transitional and the more mature. Object relations based on a transitional mode acknowledge the existence of an object outside of the self, but its separateness from the self is denied by magical illusion. To some extent this mode of relating persists in all people and exists side by side with a more mature mode of object relationships where the object is clearly delimited from the subject. Although the transitional object relationship is in a certain sense an illusion—in that the qualities of the object are created by the subject—nevertheless, the object remains a source of gratification. Although the object is created by the subject, it is still an object; it is something which the self requires for its safety. The treatment of borderline and schizophrenic patients has taught us that the therapist is of enormous significance for the patient. It is as if the patient's safety in the

---

3 The recent attempts to induce hallucinations experimentally by means of what has been called sensory deprivation is, I believe, an experimental production of object deprivation. The contact with objects of the environment can, of course, only be maintained through the senses, and when an attempt is made to block sensation artificially by means of blindfolds, cotton swathing, etc., this "sensory deprivation" also blocks the perception by means of which object relations are maintained. The experiences of Captain Slocum and Manry indicate that it is not sensory deprivation as such that is significant, for they must have been exposed to a continual influx of intense sensation in their battle with the sea.

world hangs by a slender thread, the bond with the therapist. His reliability as an object is of paramount concern, despite the fact that his separateness is only partly acknowledged. These people may distort reality, they may feel intense hatred for reality and attempt to transform it in accordance with their wishes; nevertheless, they retain an *interest* in it. I gave as an example in the previous chapter the woman who at times developed delusions that her husband had been masturbating. He at times was misidentified as her hated mother, but she maintained *interest* in him. I indicated then that it is possible to discern a nosological category—some borderline and schizophrenic people maintain interests in objects and in "reality" although they may hate it (Bion, 1959), whereas others attempt to reconstruct a new and more gratifying reality by means of hallucinations. Freud (1924a) stated:

> In a psychosis the transforming of reality is carried out upon the psychical precipitates of former relations to it—that is, upon the memory traces, ideas and judgments which have been previously derived from reality and by which reality was represented in the mind. But this relation was never a closed one; it was continually being enriched and altered by fresh perceptions. Thus the psychosis is also faced with the task of procuring for itself perceptions of a kind which shall correspond to the new reality; and this is most radically effected by means of hallucination [p. 185].

There are some people who are psychotic in that their predominant mode of loving is transitional—they have not accepted the separateness of others and they attempt to transform the world and their loved objects in accordance with their ambivalent omnipotent wishes. But these people have not formed a *substitute* for reality by means of hallucinations or a delusional system. There are those in another category who do for varying lengths of time "break" with reality and find a substitute for relationships with other people by means of hallucinations.[4]

Certain religious institutions are analogous to our own nosological distinctions. Max Weber has contrasted the ascetic, such as the Puritan, and the mystic (Weber, 1922). The ascetic may hate reality and try to transform it according to his own wishes, yet he maintains an active interest in it; the mystic flees from the world and attempts to find gratification by means of contemplation of his own inner life. What is fundamental is the different *relation* to reality.

The capacity to create a more gratifying environment by means of hallucinations is a function that is restricted to some schizophrenics. Why this is true for some schizophrenics and not for others is still unclear (Modell, 1958). However, even though the withdrawal from the environment may be massive, it is never complete. The immediate motive for the suspension or withdrawal of interest in external objects is as Freud (1940a) described:

> Namely, that the precipitating cause of the outbreak of a psychosis is either that reality has become intolerably painful or that the instincts have become extraordinarily intensified [p. 201].

The intensification of instinct refers to the aggressive instinct, which may also be experienced as a failure to differentiate loving from destructive urges (Fairbairn, 1940). That is, the individual's relation to reality appears to be suspended when he fears that he will destroy the objects in the world or in turn fears that he will be destroyed. Withdrawal of this sort may be momentary or may be relatively permanent. The following example illustrates the process of transitory hallu-

4 This other (hallucinated) group may at other times maintain interest in external objects. The nosological distinction is based on the fact that there are some psychotic people who always maintain interest in external objects, who never hallucinate or create a stable delusional system.

cination. This patient had been hospitalized for several years but experienced hallucinations only intermittently. He was playing ping-pong in a hospital ward with a competitive older man. Our patient was then taunted by a bystander, a husky Negro, who said, "I did not think you were the athletic type." At this precise moment our patient experienced an uncontrollable, murderous rage. Voices suddenly returned, saying, "That black bastard." They also said, "We will not persist—we will go away." The voices did in fact go away, for the entire episode took place in a very short period of time, probably a few minutes. It would appear that a sudden and immediate massive shift occurred in the patient's relationship to objects in the external world, and that the motive for this "break" with reality was the patient's fear of his murderous rage and his dread of retaliation.

In other patients the "break" with reality is not transitory. Hallucinations may last for months, even years, and sometimes for the rest of the patient's life. In the following illustration, the hallucinations function as a substitute for human love relationships that have been lost.

Case Illustration

The case now to be presented is taken from an earlier investigation of the phenomenology of hallucinations (Modell, 1958). I had the clinical impression, which I was able to confirm by this more careful, extensive study, that hallucinatory experiences in schizophrenia were not, as was formerly thought, predominantly critical. A stereotyped notion developed in clinical psychiatry that the predominant function of voices in schizophrenia was to accuse, that is, that the voices functioned primarily as an externalized conscience. This view proved to be one-sided. For I was able to observe that the voices had a much broader function. As Freud had suggested, the ego's relationship to actual external objects is re-created in the hallucinatory experience. The hallucination re-creates elements of both the wished-for and the actual experience with parental objects. Experiences and wishes from many stages of development are condensed by means of the immediate perceptual experience of the hallucination, very much as the dream work during sleep condenses elements from many different stages of development. For example, certain aspects of the hallucinatory experience were reminiscent of the stage of transitional object relations in that the voices performed certain executant functions—they would help the patient pronounce words, give hints on sewing and cooking, etc. These functions are reminiscent of certain functions performed by the mother that later become incorporated within the ego. Other aspects of the hallucinatory experience suggest that wishes arising from later developmental periods were gratified. (The quotes from the patient in the following sections are taken verbatim from the tape recording.)

This patient was a thirty-year-old woman who had been chronically psychotic (although she had been hospitalized only during periods of hallucinatory excitement). As far as could be determined, she had been hearing voices for at least a year and a half. These voices were described as "a man in my left ear" and "a woman in my right ear." The onset of the voices coincided with a gradual withdrawal from her husband, so that the hallucinatory experience seemed to be a substitute for the loss of her love relationship with her husband. I wish to present certain salient facts that relate directly to the content of the hallucinatory experience. This woman had suffered severe early deprivation; her parents separated during her early infancy, her mother left her in the care of the maternal grandmother. Her father, who was alcoholic and who left the family shortly after her birth, did, however, see her at infrequent intervals. There was some confirmation from others that the father was at times actually sexually seductive to her; during puberty he was observed to fondle her breasts. The significance of these facts can be seen in relation to the content of the hallucinatory experiences. The mother who deserted her is now replaced by a female voice who is constantly with her and is, the patient thinks, especially employed to watch over her. The sexually seductive father is replaced by a male voice with whom she can experience sexual excitation with a minimum of guilt, as she assumes no responsibility for the voices.

Although the patient did not directly identify the voices, it was clear from the context of her associations that they could be identified with her parents. The parental figures so reconstructed in the hallucinatory experience contained elements of both the actual and the wished-for relationships. The male voice is described as a constant companion, lover, and friend. "I wish the man would come and talk to me instead of being in my ear all the time. That makes you feel guilty—he has been with me since I came out of the hospital. I don't want him in my bathroom but if he came in and wanted to talk to me on my couch I would be glad to talk to him. I would spend the whole day with him if he wanted me."

The mother who, you will recall, had in reality rejected the patient, was perceived as a woman "who wears pants," whose real wish was to "blow" her. The maternal aspect of the relationship with the female voice was indicated by the fact that the female voice at times expressed tender concern, asking, "Did you move your cuckies?" (meaning, "Did you move your bowels?").

She believed that both the male and female voices shared her sexual experiences while she was having intercourse with her husband. For example, the male voice "normalized" her so that she obtained the orgasm that she never had with her husband. "It makes me feel like Spanish Fly. It makes me feel bad. I couldn't block them out. There wasn't anything I could do about it. They make me feel bad just the same."

Although the patient denied that the female voice directly produced genital sensations, she did explain that it was this woman's wish to "blow" her and felt that this woman passively experienced the same vaginal sensations as she did while she was having intercourse with her husband. "It just dawned on me that woman should not have so much interest in me at night . . . my mother wouldn't be interested in me and my feelings. *My mother wouldn't stand behind me and listen* [during intercourse]. That's too much. That's going too far. A woman shouldn't be that interested in another man's wife. I can see a man but not a woman. She likes me too much. I don't get it."

The male voice aroused her to sexual excitation. The erotization of sound is prominent. The patient reacted to these sounds with a mixture of anxiety and excitement. She tried to ward off the stimulation by blocking her ears. "I didn't know but I didn't want to listen. It was just the sound of a certain person's voice that gave me pleasure. I was scared when it all first started so I was trying to blank them out and I kept pushing them back because I didn't want to hear them. I just didn't want to and I kept blocking my ears. I was scared. I really was."

Although we have focused on the instinctual wishes relating to the primal scene, other more primitive wishes are condensed. For example, the patient experienced the gratification of believing that the voices were exclusively concerned with her, that is, in another sense the voices re-created a one-to-one, dyadic relationship.

The female voice was the source of much complicated advice; it advised her how to sew and cook and gave her instructions while shopping, etc. These are especially feminine activities. Although the patient follows the voice's advice, she resents it as an "interference." "When I make mistakes, she is right with me. She gets too impatient with me, and I try to figure out something all by myself. I am trying to make a clothespin apron, and she is right there with me and she is trying to tell me what to do. The fellow leaves me alone. She is a little bit too overanxious. I want to be left alone. If I asked her for help, it would be different, but I don't want her bothering me."

Freud's Concept of Object Loss and Restitution in Schizophrenia

In considering the ego's relation to objects and to reality in schizophrenia, I have suggested that there are two relatively distinct nosological groups. In one, the interest in objects and reality is maintained; in the other, there is a flight from reality, and a substitution for reality.

Originally, Freud considered only the latter group, believing withdrawal was fundamental in schizophrenia. He thought that the schizophrenic was incapable of maintaining love relationships and hence was incapable of transference. There is now general agreement amongst psychoanalysts that Freud was in this instance in error. However, some analysts still question the existence of schizophrenic withdrawal, suggesting that there is no fundamental difference between the capacity to maintain love relations in the neurotic and the psychotic person. The differences that do exist are understood as the reflection of "differing degrees of ego and instinctual regression" (Arlow and Brenner, 1964).[5] Freud's original view was one-sided; and those observers who now wish to deny that massive withdrawal occurs in schizophrenia are, I believe, also one-sided.

Freud's major essay on schizophrenia (1911b) was based upon his interpretation of the published autobiography of a distinguished German jurist, Daniel Paul Schreber. Schre-

---

[5] "Moreover, it seems more accurate to speak of defensive disturbances in various ego functions in psychosis rather than to consider a break with reality or a loss of object relations to be a universal and distinguishing feature of the onset of such conditions." (Quoted from Arlow and Brenner, 1964, p. 157.)

ber's autobiography was originally published in 1902, and
Freud's interpretation of the memoir appeared in 1911.
Schreber is probably the best-known schizophrenic in modern
psychiatry, as a voluminous literature has enveloped the psy-
chopathological material originally presented in his autobiography (see Macalpine and Hunter, 1955).

Freud paid special attention to Schreber's delusion of experiencing "the end of the world," which was interpreted as
the psychic reflection of the withdrawal of libido from people, and from the external world generally. Schreber's extreme hypochondriacal complaints and his megalomanic
self-inflation, Freud saw as indications that the libido that had
been withdrawn from objects had been invested in the ego.
This observation led to an important reformulation of psychoanalytic theory which appeared in a paper *On Narcissism*
(Freud, 1914):

> Patients of this kind, whom I have proposed to term para-
> phrenics, display two fundamental characteristics: megalo-
> mania and diversion of their interests from the external
> world—from people and things. In consequence of the latter
> change, they become inaccessible to the influence of psycho-
> analysis and cannot be cured by our efforts. But the para-
> phrenic's turning away from the external world needs to be
> more precisely characterized. A patient suffering from hys-
> teria or obsessional neurosis has also, as far as his illness
> extends, given up his relation to reality. But analysis shows
> that he has by no means broken off his erotic relations to
> people and things. He still retains them in fantasy; i.e., he
> has, on the one hand, substituted for real objects imaginary
> ones from his memory or has mixed the latter with the for-
> mer; and on the other hand, he has renounced the initiation
> of motor activities for the attainment of his aims in con-
> nection with these objects. Only to this condition of the
> libido may we legitimately apply the term 'introversion' of
> the libido which is used by Jung indiscriminately. It is other-

> wise with the paraphrenic. He seems really to have with-
> drawn his libido from people and things in the external
> world without replacing them by others in fantasy. When he
> does so replace them, the process seems to be a secondary
> one and to be part of an attempt at recovery, designed to
> lead the libido back to objects [p. 74].

Freud appears to contrast the "restitutive" symptoms of the
schizophrenic with the fantasy products of the neurotic. He
suggests that in the neurotic the fantasy is a substitute for the
object and that the hallucinatory experience in the psychotic
represents an attempt to reestablish love relations.

Freud's own clinical experience with schizophrenia we
know now was quite limited. This is one instance, I believe,
where Freud was simply wrong. Our own observations cannot support Freud's concept of restitution. Auditory hallucinations, in our opinion, are not an attempt to reestablish
relations with objects, but an attempt to find a *substitute*
for external objects. Hallucinations are an indication that
there has been a loss of a love relationship. Whether or
not objects are regained is determined by other factors and
is not a consequence of the hallucinatory process itself. (Modell, 1960). Freud was not dogmatic on this point, for in a
later paper he expressed a view that comes closer to our own
observations—that hallucinations serve as a substitute for
the perceptions of the external world (Freud, 1924a).

Although Freud believed that hallucinations may substitute for the perception of the external world, he did not
consider that hallucinations were substitutes for objects that
had been lost. However, in the paper *The Unconscious*
(1915a), Freud suggested that the verbal representation of the
object in schizophrenia serves as a substitute for the object
itself.

Freud's concept of the "object" in this particular paper
deserves closer attention, for, as we discussed in Chapter V,
the concept of "object" is derived in part from academic rep-

resentational psychology—the representation of the object is a "thing in itself." Freud believed that this representation in turn becomes linked with the word that denotes the external object. He called the original "representation," the "unconscious thing representation." According to Freud, the withdrawal of interest from external objects was represented in the mind as a "loss of the unconscious representation of the object," that is, a loss of the primal mental representation of the external object—the "unconscious thing representation." However, he noted that the words that once denoted the object are used by the schizophrenic as substitutes for the object that has been lost.

Freud has combined accurate clinical observation of the fact that the words in schizophrenia become substitutes for the things that they denote, with a theory of object representation that was borrowed almost entirely from philosophy. We cannot accept this formulation as a descriptive theory of object relations in schizophrenia, if we interpret "the unconscious representation of the object" to mean the representation of the object in the inner world. This, as we have taken pains to show, is not lost in schizophrenic withdrawal. We have arrived at the very opposite conclusion—the relation to external objects may be lost in schizophrenia, but the unconscious representation of the object is retained.

The Concept of "Internal Objects"

We have attempted to show that the internal (endopsychic) world, can, under certain circumstances, provide gratification that is analogous to the gratification afforded by external objects. The hallucinated voice, a product of the inner world, functions in a manner analogous to an external love object and, therefore, may be termed an "internal" object. However, all sources of gratification from the inner world do not necessarily function as substitutes for love objects. For example, the gratification afforded by fantasies does not necessarily indicate that there has been a loss of interest in other people or that the fantasy itself substitutes for an object. It would make little sense to describe fantasies per se as "internal objects." Only under certain circumstances does the inner world serve as a substitute for other love relationships. Melanie Klein and her students take, I believe, a somewhat broader view of the concept of the internal object.[6] This is Melanie Klein's definition of an internal object, taken from her paper, "Mourning: Its Relation to Manic-Depressive States" (1940):

> Along with the child's relation, first to his mother and soon to his father and other people, go these processes of internalization on which I have laid so much stress in my work. The baby, having incorporated his parents, feels them to be live people inside his body in a concrete way in which deep unconscious fantasies are experienced—they are, in his mind, 'internal' or 'inner' objects as I have termed them [p. 312].

We cannot dispute the fact that a baby may have a fantasy that his parents are live people inside his body, but the crucial issue is the *use* to which the fantasy is put, that is, whether or not it can be used as a *substitute* for his relation to external objects. Klein in this instance confuses descriptive and theoretic language (Zetzel, 1956b).

It can be seen that we are now approaching the problems of placing our description within a framework of theory. This is the problem that will occupy our attention in the remaining chapters.

[6] The concept of the internal object is also central to Fairbairn's theory of object relations. Fairbairn, however, also criticizes Klein for her attempt to equate fantasy with psychic structure (Fairbairn, 1952, p. 154): "Melanie Klein has never satisfactorily explained how fantasies of incorporating objects orally can give rise to the establishment of internal objects as endopsychic structures—and, unless they are such structures, they cannot properly be spoken of as internal objects at all, since otherwise they will remain mere figments of fantasy."

Chapter VIII

TOPOGRAPHIC REGRESSION AND STRUCTURAL ALTERATION: A THEORETICAL MODEL FOR THE DESCRIPTION OF OBJECT RELATIONS

The reader may have become aware that we have been using two different modes of conceptualizing the ego's relation to the environment and to reality; one relates to structure and the other to function. In earlier chapters we have emphasized that the ego's testing of reality is the outcome of the development of certain psychic structures—the development of the autonomous perceptual functions that permit the distinction between self and objects, and the development of the sense of identity that enables the acceptance of knowledge gained from perception. The sense of identity results from an ego structure but is not to be equated with the ego as a whole (Hartmann, 1950, p. 85). The sense of self is, as we have noted, *relatively* stable—it is subject to regression and progression in the sense that it is continually enriched, from adolescence onwards, by means of group identifications. Further, each new love relationship can serve to enrich the sense of self by means of a new identification with the beloved. These identifications serve to sort out and organize different sectors of "reality."

As a counterclaim to this structural conception we have also described a hypothetical organization within the ego,

121

spoken of tentatively as a "Janus-faced" organization that corresponds in some fashion to the source of gratification— whether gratification is sought by means of direct action upon the environment, or whether memories and images are used as substitutes for the gratification anticipated from actual persons. We must remind the reader that we are using the term "gratification" in a broader sense to include not only the wish for sensuous pleasure but also the wish for punishment. The inner world performs a function that is analogous to the punishment dream that Freud also saw as an extension of the dream wish.

This division also corresponds to the mode of *representation* of the environment—whether the representation is in accord "with objects as they are," that is, in accord with "reality," or whether the representation is symbolically manipulated in accordance with instinctual and defensive needs. We have, therefore, been attempting to portray the ego's relation to the environment by means of two separate metaphors, one structural and the other functional.

The functional and the structural points of view are incomplete if taken separately; what is needed is a theoretical model that will permit the juxtaposition of the functional and structural variables. To anticipate our thesis, we shall describe the relation between structure and function with the following formula: *The same structures may be used for different functions at different times.*

Now models of this sort are, in Freud's words, "intellectual scaffolding," that is, they are scientific metaphors, useful only as a method whereby something unfamiliar is placed in the context of something more familiar. As Freud was at pains to state, models are scientific fictions, not to be taken too seriously and not to be taken as a "thing itself." Models are abstractions suggested by observation, but not actually a summation of the observations themselves. Of necessity they involve idealization of the data.

In' order to describe the complexity of the human mind, some system of idealization was needed, analogous to the physicist's ability to specify initial conditions. Freud's genius provided us with a variety of models of the mental apparatus that perform the function of idealizing observation so that the natural phenomena may in some ways be ordered. As we have said, Freud did not take his own models too seriously; he would employ and discard metaphors in accordance with the task at hand. However, it is important for the nonspecialist reader to know the two major forms that Freud's metaphorical psychical apparatus has taken—the topographic and the structural. (For an extensive discussion see Gill [1963] and Arlow and Brenner [1964].) The topographic model was introduced in the theoretical section of Freud's *The Interpretation of Dreams* (1900). It was essentially "a thought experiment," an attempt to impose order upon observation by means of abstract principles analogous to Galileo's thought experiments.[1] For Freud, however, verbal language, that is, the abstraction obtained through verbal metaphor, was needed to perform the service of the mathematical language that Galileo used. The principal observable phenomena for which the model was employed were the formation of dreams and the process of repression in the neurosis. The principal conceptual abstractions that Freud derived from these observations were the concept of regulation of instinctual discharge by means of defensive barriers and the relation between the qualities of consciousness and unconsciousness. He employed a spatial metaphor, dividing the mind into systems along the lines of a reflex arc, with a sensory input separated from a motor output. This metaphor had its roots in a neurophysiological model in that it employed a concept of dis-

[1] Von Weizsacker (1964) contrasts Aristotle to Galileo, observing that Aristotle was too empirical in that he wanted to preserve nature, to save the phenomena, whereas Galileo had the courage to describe the world as we do *not* experience it.

placeable charge, a cathexis of varying intensity. However, Freud was explicit that the spatial analogy, that is, the concept of systems, was not intended to correspond to brain structure. By means of the concept of cathexis Freud was able to describe a directional or sequential relation between the systems and also to introduce a quantitative element. According to this schema three systems were designated: unconscious (Ucs), preconscious (Pcs), and conscious (Cs).[2] Freud (1900) states in *The Interpretation of Dreams*:

> Accordingly, we will picture the mental apparatus as a compound instrument, to the components of which we will give the name of 'agencies,' or (for the sake of greater clarity) 'systems.' It is to be anticipated, in the next place, that these systems may perhaps stand in a regular spatial relation to one another, in the same kind of way in which the various systems of lenses in a telescope are arranged behind one another. Strictly speaking, there is no need for the hypothesis that the psychical systems are actually arranged in a *spatial* order. It would be sufficient if a fixed order were established by the fact that in a given psychical process the excitation passes through the systems in a particular *temporal* sequence. In other processes the sequence may perhaps be a different one; that is a possibility that we shall leave open. For the sake of brevity we will in future speak of the components of the apparatus as Ψ-'systems' [pp. 536-537].

As Freud's psychoanalytic experience deepened, the relation between the unconscious and the conscious mind was no longer the major set of observations for which a model of the mind was employed. This change reflected a shift in interest from symptoms, which proved to be transitory, to the analysis of character, which proved to be more abiding and tenacious. Lifting the barrier of repression through interpre-

[2] This is of necessity an oversimplified presentation. For a more detailed account, see Gill (1963).

tations, that is, making the unconscious conscious, was not in itself sufficient to effect clinical change. For Freud became increasingly aware of the power of the forces of resistance, especially the significance of unconscious guilt. As the forces that opposed the emergence of the unconscious impulse were observed to be themselves unconscious, the distinction between conscious and unconscious thought became less significant. What became more significant were the abiding, stubborn, persistent qualities of personality. In 1923 the systems Ucs, Pcs, and Cs were replaced by the structures id, ego and superego. That is not to say that there is a simple equivalence between the topographic and structural theories; there was a major shift in Freud's entire mode of conceptualization.

There is a current debate amongst the scholars of the history of psychoanalysis regarding the relationship between topographic and structural theory. Some propose that Freud had intended the structural model to replace the topographic model, while others suggest that the topographic metaphor can be incorporated within the later structural model. It is irrelevant to our present purposes to enter into this debate. Whether Freud abandoned or retained the topographic metaphor is a problem for the history of psychoanalysis; precedent need not limit the choice of metaphor.

The focus of clinical interest has again shifted since Freud's 1923 experience—the problems of resistance and ego defenses are now well-known. The area of clinical experience that awaits better conceptualization is that of disturbed human object relationships. What is now needed is a model that would better conceptualize the ego's relationship to the environment and would encompass progressive and regressive alterations in object relations.

We suggest that alteration of function and structure requires two different but interrelated modes of conceptualization. For this reason we wish to retain a topographic metaphor applied to *functional* alterations within the ego, while maintaining the structural metaphor to represent the more or less abiding configurations within the ego that are the result of developmental (historical) processes. This does not mean that we intend to use Freud's topographic theory as it was described in *The Interpretation of Dreams* and in his paper *On the Unconscious*. It is rather that we wish to apply certain ways of thinking that Freud used to our problem of describing alterations of object relations. Principal amongst these ways of thinking is the notion of cathexis, that is, a charge that has an intensity and direction, and by implication some concept of quantity and spatial arrangement. This is purely an imaginary model; it is simply an aid to conceptualization. Those readers who do not prefer a spatial analogy can substitute for a spatial notion a concept of sequentiality. We intend to develop certain intellectual tools in order to describe changes along a certain dimension or parameter.[3]

I have described the functional organization within the ego as Janus-faced. *One portion of the ego* is organized to obtain gratification from the external world and corresponds to what Freud termed the reality ego; another portion obtains gratification from within and can be tentatively termed the inner world.

When we speak of portions of the ego, we are already using

---

[3] The term "regression" has long been employed to signify change along a given parameter. It is not an ideal term as it carries with it the implication of something infantile and maladaptive—it has, in short, acquired judgmental overtones. There is, however, some justification for retaining it as a description of topographic change. However, the term "regression" as applied to concepts of psychic structure is, in certain instances, inaccurate. For example, the failure to develop a sense of identity may not represent regression from a higher level of development, as a higher level may never have been achieved. In this instance we are describing not a regression but an arrest in development. In other instances, such as may occur in acute schizophrenia, where there can be a complete dissolution of a fragile sense of identity, one can properly call this a regression. For these reasons I have employed the more inclusive term "alteration" rather than "regression" when describing changes in psychic structure.

a spatial metaphor.[4] As Freud said, with regard to the development of the topographic model in *The Interpretation of Dreams,* one can, if one wishes, replace the notion of systems organized in space if one wants to think of the systems organized in some sequential order. This is all that we are attempting to do when we speak of a topographic metaphor.

If we then consider that *there are two functional systems within the ego corresponding to the source from which gratification is achieved, we can then conceptualize a shift of interest from the outer to the inner world as a shift in cathexis from the outer to the inner portions of the ego* (see also Sandler and Rosenblatt, 1962, p. 132). Now, the term cathexis is an imaginary concept, a metaphor, involving a notion of intensity and direction, that is, of a charge analogous to electricity. Its utility resides in the fact that directional and quantitative alterations can be simultaneously noted. *Topographic regression can then be defined as a shift in cathexis from the external to the internal world.* A quantitative element is implied. Such abstract psychic models have a tendency to become divorced from the data to which they are addressed, so that we shall now try to employ this model to differentiate object relations in the neurosis and psychosis.

Topographic Regression without Significant Structural Alteration—Neurotic States

Let us attempt to use this model to describe the development of the transference neurosis in psychoanalytic treatment. Let us imagine an ideal instance, that is, the so-called

---

[4] Those authors who wish to completely substitute structural for topographic theory claim that Freud abandoned using a spatial metaphor. However, Freud states in *An Outline of Psychoanalysis* (p. 161): "The process of something becoming conscious is above linked with the perceptions which our sense organs receive from the external world. From the topographical point of view, therefore, it is a phenomenon which takes place in the *outermost cortex of the ego*" (italics added). When Freud speaks of an outermost cortex he is making use of a spatial metaphor.

"classical" neurosis, with no significant regression of ego structure. The technique of psychoanalysis was designed to induce a form of regression that serves to activate childhood fantasies and, if successful, to recapitulate the infantile neuroses and their relationship to the analyst. The perceptual world of the patient is limited by the use of the couch; he does not see the analyst and accordingly, there is a shift of attention from the world of outer reality to the world of inner reality.

Freud (1912) described the development of transference as follows:

> Let us picture the psychological situation during the treatment. An invariable and indispensable precondition of *every* onset of a psychoneurosis is the process to which Jung has given the appropriate name of 'introversion.' That is to say: the portion of the libido which is capable of becoming conscious and is directed towards reality is diminished, and the portion which is directed *away* from reality and is unconscious, and which, though it may still feed the subject's fantasies, nevertheless belongs to the unconscious, is proportionately increased [p. 102].

What Freud described by means of a purely instinctual conceptualization in that early paper can now be schematically represented as a cathectic shift from the outer to the inner world. That is to say, a topographic regression. The patient becomes preoccupied with fantasies and with the revival of earlier memories and earlier identifications. We have schematically represented a differentiating organization within the ego in terms of function—whether gratification is sought from within or from without. The sequence of topographic regression in psychoanalytic treatment consisting of the cathexis of infantile imagoes does not represent simply a withdrawal of interest from the outer to the inner world; as the transference neurosis develops there is an intense interest in the person of the analyst. *Using a topographic meta-phor we can describe two steps in this sequence: first, the cathectic shift from the reality ego to the inner world; second, a cathectic shift from the inner world back to the reality ego —gratification is sought from the outer world in the person of the analyst.* However, with the initial cathectic shift from the outer world to the inner world that accompanies a topographic regression, a change has occurred in the perception of the outer world. The development of the transference neurosis is an attempt to re-create in the outer world the contents of the inner world. You will recall Freud's illustration of the little boy who, in response to his mother's departure, played a game consisting of throwing a spool behind the curtain of his cot. His mother, who left him, was symbolically represented in the internal world by a spool that could be manipulated at will. The painful event was re-created but with an illusion of mastery. This is a paradigm of the transference neurosis. The pain experienced in relation to external objects is dealt with by a symbolic re-creation in the inner world of the relation between self and objects, a re-creation that is altered in accordance with defensive and instinctual needs. An element of magic is retained, as it was in the little boy's game. By symbolic manipulation, an illusion of control and mastery is created—an illusion that the original objects in the external world can be controlled by means of the symbolic representation in the internal world. In the transference neurosis, this internal reality is transferred upon the external reality, that is, upon the relationship with the analyst. It is not only that the analyst is perceived in accordance with older imagoes, he is also unconsciously manipulated to *act* in accordance with these imagoes so that the analytic process itself becomes a stage for the re-creation of the internal drama.

It is not my intention to discuss here in detail the well-known development of the transference neurosis but simply to use it as an illustration of topographic regression—*the contents of the inner world invade or interpenetrate the reality ego.* There is an intense search for gratification from the external world, but the structuring of the perception of the external world has been altered in accordance with the contents of the inner world.

A transference neurosis is to be sure a special form of human relationship. It is a unique relationship created by the aims and purpose of the psychoanalytic encounter. However, all love objects are perceived to some extent in accordance with the contents of the inner world. To describe the process schematically: Where there is topographic regression, the effects of this regression will be experienced by the reality ego as well. When there is a cathectic shift from the outer to the inner world, the symbolic contents of the inner world interpenetrate that portion of the ego facing outward. This observation is not confined to psychoanalysis but, expressed in different terms, is the foundation of Cassirer's concept of knowledge of the external world. I quote from Cassirer's monumental work, *The Philosophy of Symbolic Forms* (1953, pp. 91–92):

> Not only science, but language, myth, art and religion as well, provide the building stones from which the world of 'reality' is constructed for us, as well as that of the human spirit, in sum the World-of-the-I. . . . In each one of its freely projected signs the human spirit apprehends the object and at the same time apprehends itself and its own formative law. And this peculiar interpenetration prepares the way for the deeper determination both of subject and object.

Cassirer's basic thesis is that apprehension of reality occurs through the mediation of symbolic forms.

The fundamental importance of this concept lies in its range of application. It refers both to man's love relations in their widest sense as well as to his creative activities and his perception of the external environment. The interrelationship between loving and creativity has been recognized outside of psychoanalysis. Love has been considered to be a creative act, in that the capacity to love is an act of the imagination. The form love assumes, however, is influenced by cultural styles as well as the act of individual creation (Singer, 1966).

We have been considering topographic regression in the (relative) absence of structural regression. This comes very close to Kris's concept of regression in the service of the ego (although Kris did not distinguish between topographic and structural regression). Kris observed (*The Psychology of Caricature,* 1935) that in aesthetic expression the ego uses the primary process for its own purposes. There he coined the felicitous phrase "regression in the service of the ego." Kris (1950) later described this process in greater detail:

> The clinical observation of creators and the study of introspective reports of experiences during creative activity tend to show that we are faced with a shift in the cathexis of certain ego functions. Thus a frequent distinction is made between an inspirational and an "elaborational" phase in creation. The inspirational phase is characterized by the facility with which id impulses, or their closer derivatives, are received. One might say that countercathectic energies to some extent are withdrawn, and added to the speed, force, or intensity with which the preconscious thoughts are formed. During the "elaborational" phase, the countercathectic barrier may be reinforced, work proceed slowly, cathexis is directed to other ego functions such as reality testing, formulation, or general purposes of communication. Alternations between the two phases may be rapid, oscillating, or distributed over long stretches of time [p. 312].

When we describe the contents of the inner world "interpenetrating" the reality ego, we do not wish to suggest that the external world is then represented entirely in accordance with internal symbolic forms. The capacity to represent objects "as they are" is retained; it is rather that an element of illusion enters into the representation of reality. Other psychoanalysts have made essentially the same point. Rycroft (1956), acknowledging the observations of Winnicott (1951) and Millner (1955), states: ". . . Unconscious symbolic processes underlie the development and maintenance of a sense of reality just as much as they do neurosis." This leads us back to the consideration of the relation of structure to function, that is, of the relation between structural and topographic regression.

Again an examination of transference in the neurosis can illustrate this problem. The relationship between the analyst and the patient does not consist solely of a transference neurosis. Parallel to the development of the infantile neurosis there is a development of a "true" object relation to the analyst (Zetzel, 1956a). That is, the patient perceives the analyst as he is "in reality" and acknowledges the mutual task upon which they are both engaged. Furthermore, the patient may identify with certain aspects of the analyst's "real" personality. He may identify with the analyst's capacity to maintain distance and objectivity, and (hopefully) may identify with the analyst's more tolerant superego. In order for the analyst's identity to be perceived and accepted, the patient's identity must also be preserved; that is, for a successful analysis and for the development of what has been termed a successful therapeutic alliance, there must be a minimum of structural regression. The analyst addresses himself to the "thou" of the patient. The aim of psychoanalytic treatment is to foster topographic regression but not a structural regression. The analyst tries to preserve, by acknowledging the "thou" of the patient, the patient's sense of identity. A successful psychoanalysis will lead to a structural progression in that the sense of identity is strengthened and enriched (Loewald, 1960).

Therefore, it is a necessary precondition for analysis that structural development proceed to the point where the sense of identity can be maintained in the face of topographic regression. This is, of course, a somewhat idealized presentation, as some degree of structural regression usually does occur in psychoanalysis. At these times there may be transitory lapses in reality testing (Loewald, 1951) that accompany transitory losses of the sense of identity. Such structural regressions are reversible. The persistence of structural organizations safeguards the function of reality testing. Although there may be a blurring of the distinction between the inner and outer worlds so that the symbolic elements of the inner world invade the representation of the outer world, the structural integrity of the sense of self preserves the capacity to separate the object from the self. The object may be perceived in accordance with qualities of the inner world —that is, an element of illusion enters into perception—but the capacity to acknowledge the separateness of the external object is maintained.

The preservation of the structural element is essential also for what Kris termed the elaborational phase of artistic creation. That is, the symbolic content of the inner world needs to be translated into the language of the beholder. In the elaborational phase the artist is concerned with communication—he must acknowledge the existence and needs of other objects. In visual art the artist must in some way address himself to the conceptual forms derived from convention, forms employed by the beholder (Gombrich, 1960). We have described some aspects of this earlier in our discussion of group identification and its relation to the structure of a segment of reality.

Kris's description of the alternation between the inspirational and elaborational phases of creativity is analogous to our description of the shift of cathexis from the inner world to the reality ego. Kris also noted that alternations between the two phases may be rapid, oscillating, or distributed over long stretches of time. Until now we have focused upon relatively rapid alternations or oscillations. There is, however, a variety of states where the cathexis of the inner world is more prolonged, and yet in a general sense, the interest in external objects is not abandoned. We are referring to the states of normal mourning and certain depressive disorders (Freud, 1917, p. 244). The existence of the object is prolonged *internally* by means of a "hypercathexis of memories and expectations"; psychoanalytic observation can confirm that the lost object is maintained in the inner world by means of an identification. A similar process occurs in some depressions where, in contrast to mourning, there is not actual loss of the loved object. In such conditions the shift from the outer to the inner world (topographic regression) does not follow an oscillatory movement as in the transference neurosis, but the inner world itself remains cathected.

In this schematic model we must refer at least in some fashion to a quantitative factor, although no possibility of measurement exists. For in the conditions we have described, normal mourning and moderate depressive disorders, a certain withdrawal of interest from objects in the external world occurs but not to the same extent as in the psychosis.

Topographic Regression with Significant Structural Alteration—Psychotic States

The structural metaphor refers to something more enduring, yet not absolutely rigid and unchanging. In a very well-known section in *The Ego and the Id*, Freud describes the ego as a "precipitate of abandoned object cathexis so that it contains the *history* of those object traces" (italics added). A historical or archeological analogy breaks down in one important sense, for in history the sense of time cannot be reversed—historical time moves in only one direction, whereas in states of structural regression the psychological past can be reevoked.[5]

When we described the development of a transference neurosis in the previous section we imagined an ideal case where there was a relative absence of structural regression. That is to say, for the most part a sense of identity was maintained. However, we know that the sense of identity, which can be conceptualized as the sign of psychic structure, is not absolutely rigid—it is continually being enriched through new identifications and is subject to constant regressive influences. We described in Chapter IV that the development of the sense of identity was the outcome of the hard-won struggle to accept the separateness of objects. The wish to abandon our identity, to give up our sense of separateness, to relinquish our unity, to again merge with other objects is always present. The achievement of the sense of self implies also a recognition that one really is in a certain sense alone in the world. This painful awareness has as its counterpoise the wish to abandon one's identity and seek fusion with other objects.

There are, however, some individuals whose sense of identity has never been fully achieved. These people compose the group of psychoses. In these individuals, too, the structural organization of the sense of self is not rigid but is subject to fluctuation. The historical development of the sense of self in these people can be said to have been foreshortened by the failure to internalize the loving, protective parental object. The sense of self, such as it does exist, does not rest

[5]"This brings us to the more general problem of preservation in the sphere of the mind. The subject has hardly been studied as yet; but it is so attractive and important that we may be allowed to turn our attention to it for a little, even though our excuse is insufficient. Since we overcame the error of supposing that the forgetting we are familiar with signified a destruction of the memory trace—that is, its annihilation—we have been inclined to take the opposite view, that in mental life nothing which has once been formed can perish—that everything is somehow preserved and that in suitable circumstances (when, for instance, regression goes back far enough) it can once more be brought to light" (Freud, 1930, p. 69).

upon "realistic" identifications but is organized instead around fantasies of omnipotence.

There are significant differences in the development of the transference in the psychotic and neurotic cases. Topographic regression may proceed along similar lines; that is, the sequential development of the topographic regression may follow the same path as we have described earlier—the cathexis may shift back again to the reality ego, carrying with it the imprint of the inner world. The difference resides in the structural organization.

In the psychotic case illustration (Chapter VI), with a (relative) absence of a coherently formed, integrated sense of self, there was an incapacity to accept the separateness of the external object and hence a failure in reality testing. When the object of the analyst is invested with the imagoes of the inner world, there is a denial of the perception of the analyst as he is—instead the projected imagoes are accepted as "reality."

The direction assumed by the topographic regression in psychosis may be such that there is a return to the reality ego and the development of an intense transference psychosis. In other instances the inner world may remain cathected, leading to a relative withdrawal from external objects.

In some instances we have been using the term "structural alteration" to refer to a developmental arrest; in other instances, however, there may be an actual undoing of psychic structure—a true regression. In certain stages of schizophrenia there may be an actual dissolution of the imperfectly formed sense of identity. It is as if the constituent elements, that is, the identifications that make up the sense of self, no matter how amorphous this sense may have been, become disintegrated. The area of religious experience again affords us a useful analogy. The losing of an old sense of identity and the finding of a new self is analogous to the experience of religious conversion—a psychic rebirth (James, 1902). In such experiences people may undergo a sudden and total change in their character and acquire in its stead a new character which may remain permanent.

We are not able to delineate further the nature of this process, for when we say the sense of self is lost, we must in some fashion refer to a process that cuts off from awareness an entire sector of organized memories. Here again the pattern of *topographic* regression is similar to that described in the neurosis, in that we can observe some patients whose cathexis remains fastened upon the inner world, and others whose cathexis returns to external objects. The pattern that topographic regression assumes is a schematic representation of the two (psychotic) nosological groups we described in an earlier chapter. There may be a persistent cathexis of the *inner world* or, conversely, a heightened interest in the external world whose objects are invested with the content of the inner world. An illustration of this latter instance would be the case described of a woman who had the delusion that her husband was masturbating. As we noted before, there was at these times a dissolution of her sense of identity and the imagoes composing the inner world were projected to real persons of the external world. The internal imagoes consisted of a depriving mother and a deprived child. The delusion that her husband masturbated was a projection of the imago of the depriving mother; that is, he was depriving her, the patient, of his body contents. In this aspect of the drama, she, the patient, was the deprived child. There was an intense interest in the objects of the external world (she hated her husband but was preoccupied with him), even though those objects were misidentified in accordance with the contents of the inner world.[6]

---

[6] The projection of inner imagoes upon an external object without appreciation of the actual qualities of the object itself, is similar to a process that the Kleinian analysts have called "projective identification."

Where the topographic regression does not follow the same sequential order as in this illustration, that is, where the topographic regression is such that the inner world remains cathected, the inner world may be used as a substitute for external objects. The clearest example of this is the development of auditory hallucinations where the experience with voices substitutes for external objects. The voices perform all the functions attributed to objects in the environment. As we have described previously the voices can be companions, critics, advisors, and the source of direct sexual gratification, leading in many instances to actual orgasm. The range of content of the symbolic representation of the inner world is broad in schizophrenia. Substitutes for objects may be found not only in the re-creation of auditory experiences, such as in voices; it may also involve the cathexis of bodily sensations or visual images.

The superimposition of structural concepts upon the topographic permits a differentiation of neurotic and psychotic withdrawal. The sequence of topographic regression may be the same, but there is an enormous difference between the fantasies of a neurotic and the hallucinations of a schizophrenic. In the former, the relation to external objects is maintained; in the latter, this relation is, more or less, abandoned and the hallucinatory experience itself is accepted as a substitute for the objects that have been lost. The crucial difference can be described as structural—the loss of the sense of identity in schizophrenia which is a testimony to the miscarriage of an earlier developmental process.

The Relation of the Concept of Topographic Regression to Freud's Concept of Ego and Object Libido

It will not escape the attention of the reader who is familiar with Freud's paper *On Narcissism* that our concept of topographic regression—a shifting of cathexis between the inner world and the reality-seeking ego—bears a familial resemblance to Freud's concept of ego libido and object libido. Freud (1914) states:

> Thus we form the idea of there being an original libidinal cathexis of the ego, from which some is later given off to objects, but which fundamentally persists and is related to the object-cathexis much as the body of an amoeba is related to the pseudopodia which it puts out. In our researches, taking, as they did, neurotic symptoms for their starting point, this part of the allocation of libido necessarily remained hidden from us at the outset. All that we noticed were the emanations of this libido—the object cathexis, which can be sent out and drawn back again. We see also, broadly speaking, an antithesis between ego-libido and object-libido. The more the one is employed, the more the other becomes depleted. The highest phase of development of which object libido is capable is seen in the state of being in love, when the subject seems to give up his own personality in favor of an object-cathexis; while we have the opposite condition in the paranoiac's phantasy (or self-perception) of the 'end of the world.' Finally, as regards the differentiation of psychical energies we are led to the conclusion that to begin with, during the state of narcissism, they exist together and that our analysis is too coarse to distinguish between them; not until there is object-cathexis is it possible to discriminate a sexual energy—the libido—from an energy of the ego instincts [p. 75].

One must remember that Freud wrote this when he was concerned primarily with his theory of instincts. He wished especially to maintain a dual instinct theory in the face of Jung's repudiation of the existence of sexual instincts (Jung suggested that libido simply represents a general psychic interest). At the time that this paper was written, Freud was employing the classifications of ego instincts and sexual instincts to correspond to the differences between the aims of self-preservation (the ego instincts) and the aim of the individual (sexual instincts). This classification was subsequently abandoned and replaced by the duality of Eros and Thanatos. Therefore, a division of libido into object and ego libido follows an abandoned classification and cannot now be maintained. Freud at this time was attempting to construct a model that would help to explicate the complex alterations of the loss of objects and reality in schizophrenia. However, he attempted to do this by placing the burden of explanation upon instinctual theory alone. Instinctual theory is clearly inadequate for this task.

Freud's use of an instinctual or purely energic metaphor in terms of a reciprocating depletion of object and ego libido has been criticized as a "hydraulic model of love." It is, I believe, the limitations of instinctual theory that have led to this criticism. Although the problem cannot be solved by instinctual theory alone, Freud was essentially correct in formulating an antithesis between the external and internal worlds. Our proposal here, one that superimposes functional and structural metaphors, is an attempt to preserve Freud's insight by uniting the energic metaphor to a concept of ego function.

The Relation of Topographic and Structural Regression to Other Metapsychological Theories

The formulation of several forms of regression occurring simultaneously along different parameters is not new. Freud (1900), in *The Interpretation of Dreams,* states:

> It is further to be remarked that regression plays a no less important part in the theory of the formation of neurotic symptoms than it does in that of dreams. Three kinds of regression are thus to be distinguished: (a) *topographical* regression, in the sense of the schematic picture of the Ψ systems, which we have explained above; (b) *temporal* regres-

sion, insofar as what is in question is a harking back to older psychical structures; and (c) *formal* regression, where primitive methods of expression and representation take the place of the usual ones. All these three kinds of regression are, however, at one at bottom and occur together as a rule; for what is older in time is more primitive in form and in psychical topography lies nearer to the perceptual end [p. 548].

Gill and Brenman (1959) also employ concepts of simultaneous regression along two parameters. The phenomenon that they describe is hypnosis. They utilize, as we have, Kris's concept of regression in the service of the ego. Gill and Brenman speak also of "the preservation of a usual ego structure" while a subsystem of the ego forms "regressive characteristics."

> We have already said that our descriptive differentiation of the two kinds of regression suggests that, structurally, in regression in the service of the ego the usual ego structure persists, but that at the same time a subsystem which has regressive characteristics is formed in the ego. It is also possible in a regression proper for a subsystem within the ego to develop subsequently [p. 202].

Gill and Brenman's differentiation of an ego "with regressive characteristics" from "regression proper within the ego" may be similar to topographic and structural regression. They, however, define regression quite differently. They have defined regression as a "loss of autonomy from the id" and a "loss of autonomy from the environment."[7]

In our description of alterations in the quality and form of

7 I have not found this specific definition to be applicable to the concept of object relations. This may suggest that as psychoanalytic knowledge advances, we may find it necessary to employ *ad hoc* models for separate phenomena, and relinquish at least for the present, a model of the psychic apparatus as a whole as if it encompasses all clinical knowledge.

object relations, we are suggesting that the same structures, that is, the outcome of a given historical development, may at different times serve different functions.[8] For example, an ego structure, the sign of which is the sense of identity, forms the basis for the acceptance of the separateness of external objects. However, where there is withdrawal of interest from the external world and an attempt to find gratification from within, the same structure may serve as a substitute for external objects. We are referring here to the narcissistically loved self.

We recognize that this theory raises many other questions. For example, are we to suppose that there are different registrations or memory systems within the ego that reflect the shift that occurs in topographic regression? Are there "realistic" self-images that are registered separately from imagoes based in part on fantasy? These issues will be considered in greater detail in the next chapter.

A Note on the Concept of Mental Content

When we speak of structural or topographic regression, we are using words that do not refer to things in the external world. Model building, as we have said earlier, is in the nature of a thought experiment. We are using words to construct a model of the *relationship* between observable things. It is unfortunate but unavoidable that the language employed in a theoretical model, that is, theoretical language, uses the same words as those applied to observation. For example, Freud used the term "cathexis" as a pure metaphor, but he also used it to refer to a description of an intensity of affect (Freud and Breuer, 1895, p. 89). The terms "primary process" and "secondary process" have had similar fates.

---

[8] Broadbent (1965) suggests something similar in a neurophysiological model of the brain: "The same components may be used for different functions at different times."

They have been used as theoretically constructed mental apparatuses to refer to portions of the mind and are also used to describe clinical phenomena. Now we have referred to mental content, such as the fantasy of omnipotence, and have suggested that such a fantasy forms a part of a mental structure, the self-image. When we refer to a fantasy in relation to mental structure, we do not necessarily intend to signify something that can be directly observed by an analyst who is treating the patient. The term "fantasy" is used in a double sense—a theoretic sense and an ostensive sense.

In this chapter we have tried to construct a model that will aid in sorting out observations concerning object relations. Such a model cannot avoid the idea of mental content. We can use the same word in two different senses if the reader is clear that this is our intent. This problem has plagued psychoanalytic theorizing. Some psychoanalysts have attempted to solve it by divorcing psychoanalytic theory from mental content; this has encouraged arid, academic theorizing. Others, such as Klein, have in part sacrificed scientific recognition by treating patients' descriptive fantasies as psychic structure (see Chapter VII). This has led to a confusion between descriptive and theoretical language, between data and inference. Unless we construct a new scientific language, we are faced with the necessity of using the same words for entirely different significations. If we remain clear about the difference between descriptive and theoretical language, we avoid the danger of what has been called "reification" of psychic structure.

Chapter IX

CONCLUSION: THE RELATION BETWEEN STRUCTURE AND FUNCTION

We have used the term "topographic regression" to refer to a different set of observations from those for which Freud had originally intended the term. Freud used the topographic concept to construct a model of the mind that would account for the difference between consciousness and unconsciousness. The observations that led to this theory were principally dreams and neurotic symptom formation; the topographic metaphor was designed to express *functional* relations between separate psychic systems. In employing the same mode of conceptualization for a different area of observation, we have not introduced anything that is essentially new but have attempted to combine several aspects of Freud's older theories in a new way, a way that would be consonant with later structural theory. The topographic metaphor permits one to describe the functional relations between separate systems by means of a concept of a cathectic charge of variable direction. By this means, sequential processes can be described. Instead of the systems that Freud employed—preconscious, conscious, and unconscious—we have considered a different functional organization according to whether gratification is sought from within the ego or from the external world. This is a functional organization in terms of the reality ego and the inner world. The sequential changes described as topographic re-

144

gression enabled us to describe the withdrawal of interest from the external world and the return of interest to the reality ego, carrying with it the organization of the inner world, that is, a return with altered signification. In this theoretical construction we have attempted to integrate a concept that Freud expressed earlier in his paper *On Narcissism,* that is, the antithesis between ego libido and object libido. We wish to integrate three separate areas of Freudian theory—the topographic metaphor, the theory of narcissism, and the theory of psychic structure. We have confined our attention to processes occurring within the ego itself, so that we have not considered the larger area of the interrelationships between the three psychic structures themselves—that is, the interrelationships between the ego, id, and superego.

One of our major assertions has been that *the same structure may serve different functions at different times.* We wish now to apply this schema to the concept of identification.

Identification

The term "identification" refers in some way to the representation of an external object that has been taken into the ego to form a *permanent* element within the total personality. Identification, therefore, is to be distinguished from imitation, a more transitory process.

Freud (1900) suggested that reality testing relied on the fact that a memory schema of the external object was established within the mind:

> Thus the aim of this first psychical activity was to produce a perceptual identity—a repetition of the perception which was linked with the satisfaction of the need [p. 566].

Reality testing consisted, in this sense, of "refinding" in the external world that which responded to the original schema. Freud (1925) referred again to this idea in his paper on *Negation:*

> The other sort of decision made by the function of judgment
> —as to the real existence of something of which there is a
> presentation (reality testing)—is a concern of the definitive
> reality ego, which develops out of the initial pleasure ego.
> It is now no longer a question of whether what has been per-
> ceived (a thing) shall be taken into the ego or not, but of
> whether something which is in the ego as a presentation
> can be rediscovered in perception (reality) as well. . . . The
> first and immediate aim, therefore, of reality testing is not to
> *find* an object in real perception which corresponds to the
> one presented, but to *refind* such an object, to convince one-
> self that it is still there [pp. 237-238].

Identification is necessary for *perception* of the object and for testing of reality. It is something which must *precede* the perception of an object. However, Freud also considered identification in a very different sense—as something that was set over against the "libidinal cathexis of objects" (Fenichel, 1926). That is, identification can be used as a substitute for an object relationship. In *Group Psychology and the Analysis of the Ego,* Freud (1921) reviewed the various concepts of identification. There he termed identification a regressive form of object relationship denoting the distinction between wanting to *be* like the object from wanting to *have* the ob-ject—that is, *identifying* with the object is an alternative and, according to Freud, a regressive alternative, to the sexual *possession* of the object.

We must, however, consider the process of identification from still other points of view. When we have related iden-tification to the process of the representation of an external object within the ego, we must consider the distinction be-tween processes that incorporate the object "as it is in reality" and processes where the object that is internalized is a creation of the subject itself.

Some of these issues have been introduced in our earlier discussion of transitional object relationships, where we stressed the child's capacity to superimpose the contents of the inner world upon the external object, that is, to create an object. The form of this creation, as we have discussed previously, corresponds to the omnipotent wish—that is, the child takes into his ego, he identifies with an external object that is invested with the qualities of omnipotence. The earliest core of identification that we can uncover in the analysis of adult patients is a core that is organized around such omnipotent fantasies. The concept of the "phallic mother" is another example of how the object taken into the ego is the creation of the subject. For we know that children of both sexes may believe that their mother is not "castrated" but does, in fact, possess a penis. This penis may be imagined as analogous to the male penis or may be thought to be hidden —in the vagina or in the anus. We are not concerned with the specific form of this fantasy, only with the fact that such a fantasy may become the nexus of an early identification— an identification that is created by the subject.

The function of this fantasy is now well understood. It is the result of anxiety. This anxiety, in turn, is the consequence of man's prolonged biological helplessness. Man's dependence upon parental objects means that his actual safety as an infant and young child is vouchsafed only by the continued presence of the protecting parental objects. The experience of helplessness, the danger of actual loss of the parental objects to which the fear of castration is added, is avoided by means of a signal of anxiety which serves to institute defensive mental mechanisms, such as denial, which, in turn, rests upon the illusion of a lack of separateness of subject and object. These processes are described by the more general term "magical thought," which embodies a belief in

action at a distance—that action upon the symbol is equivalent to action upon the object denoted by the symbol. The
essence of magical belief is that the acknowledged perceptual
separation of objects is mere appearance. The magical object
created by the subject becomes, in turn, part of the subject's
own ego. That is, the form given by the ego to objects in
the external environment becomes reflected back into the
ego itself by means of identification.

Anxiety results, however, not only from the possibility of
actual separation but also from the pressure of instinctual
tensions, tensions which the child perceives as threatening
his relationship with the parental object (Freud, 1926). It is
in accord with the child's magical thinking to believe that
effects are measured by the intensity of feeling. That is,
the angrier one feels, the greater the destructive effect of one's
rage, and the greater need to rely upon magical belief to
mitigate the danger of actual loss of parental objects.

The creation of the object by means of the subject has
been of special interest to Melanie Klein and her students.
(We have criticized Klein's use of the concept of fantasy in
Chapter VIII.) I have observed in borderline and schizophrenic patients the same fantasies that Klein described.
However, I, along with many other American colleagues,
cannot accept her explanations. Mrs. Klein has described the
splitting of the self-created object as the result of two early
developmental processes that she terms the paranoid and
depressive position. In contrast to Freud's more general considerations of the motives for the institution of anxiety
(Freud considered a complementary series, consisting of
actual object loss as well as the effect of an increase of instinctual tension), Klein believes the motive for anxiety is simple
and singular—the death instinct. She thinks that the infantile
ego is in danger of disintegration unless it can extrude, that
is, project, parts of itself onto the maternal object which
then is perceived as a persecutor (Klein, 1946). This is called

the "paranoid position." At a somewhat later stage, a secondary process issues, in that the external maternal object itself must be preserved. The object is "split" into "good and bad portions," both parts of which become the nexus for omnipotent identifications. This is called the depressive position. The depressive position denotes a concern for the object and a need to preserve it, in contrast to the earlier paranoid position where there is a need for the ego to rid itself of its own "badness." Although remnants of such fantasies can be observed in adult patients, I find it impossible to accept Klein's assertions that these processes occur shortly after birth. She has unfortunately detracted from the credibility of her own contribution by her insistence that object relations occur at birth, thus attributing a complexity to the mind of the newborn that receives no confirmation from the observations of Piaget, Spitz, and others, who observe a gradual unfolding of autonomous maturational processes.

To return then to the more general consideration of identifications, what is taken into the ego as an identification may not represent an object of the external world as it is viewed by other observers, that is, as it is in "reality," but what is taken in may represent the object as "created" by the subject. The motive force for this creation is anxiety, as we have described, and the defensive processes of extrusion and incorporation are synonymous with the terms "projection" and "introjection."

However, all identifications that are the result of defensive needs, that is, the result of processes instituted by anxiety, are not "created by the subject." An identification may be defensive, yet correspond to the "real qualities of the object." If one is frightened by an object, one may identify with the object that is feared; this process, "identification with the aggressor," can be commonly observed in young children. Anna Freud (1936) describes it as follows:

> By impersonating the aggressor, assuming his attributes or imitating his aggression, the child transforms himself from the person threatened into the person who makes the threat [p. 113].

This identification with aspects of the frightening parent may become a facet of the individual's character. The qualities in question are not created by the subject but "exist" in the object.

If we consider identifications from the standpoint of function, we may discern two broad categories. Identifications may serve the function of "refinding" the object in the external world, that is, the perception and structuring of reality, or identifications may serve the *functions of the inner world*. The functions of the inner world, although interrelated, may be summarized as follows: (1) Objects may be taken into the ego in order to preserve the external object; that is, the negative or painful attributes of the object may be assumed by the subject in order to preserve or "idealize" the object (see Rycroft, 1955). (2) Objects may be taken into the ego in order to substitute for the gratification of external objects. (3) Objects may be taken into the ego to remove, by means of magical control, the painful or dangerous qualities of the external objects by identification with the aggressor. At first glance it might appear that the first and the third examples are identical. In both instances, one wishes to remove something that is painful or dangerous in the external object and take it into the internal world in order to control it. However, in the first instance, when we speak of identification in order to idealize the object, the wish is to preserve the "goodness" of the object at the expense of taking the "badness" of the object into the self. This is a common mechanism in depression. In the third instance the aim is not to *preserve* the object but to *control* the object. These distinctions are made only for purposes of exposition, whereas in actuality all these functions are interrelated.

It would be a mistake to believe that the functional aspects of identification as we have just described them are limited to the earliest years of human development. Vestiges of the same process can be observed in the adult. For example, a man of forty-five accepted his wife's dominance and needed to believe in her competence and reliability. When this woman developed a paranoid disorder and began to show marked errors in judgment, the husband preserved his illusions concerning his wife by means of an identification. He believed that *he* was going crazy and thus denied to consciousness any perception of his wife's developing illness. This would be an instance of an object taken into the ego in order to preserve it.

There are, as we have noted, other parallel functions of identifications that serve the reality ego and prepare for direct action upon the environment. For example, Hendrick (1951) described the child's identification with partial executant ego functions of the mother. A child identifies with the mother's way of doing certain things. So that ego identifications of this sort contribute largely to a growing capacity to deal effectively with the external world. Hendrick believed that this form of identification occurred prior to the development of superego identifications. He suggested that identifications could be further classified according to the specific structural system into which they become integrated, that is, whether they become part of the ego or superego.

To recapitulate: Identifications may be considered from the standpoint of (1) functional considerations—whether they serve the inner world or the reality ego; (2) historical considerations—the specific critical phase of development during which they are initiated; and (3) structural considerations —whether they become part of a specific system, such as the ego or superego.

Throughout this work we have noted that identifications serve two different functions. In one sense identifications serve to refind the object—that is, identifications are the necessary precondition for the finding of the object in the external world and so are a precondition for knowledge of the external world. In this sense an identification is thought to be some form of semipermanent schemata analogous to memory but not restricted to memory, since the schemata can also be altered by instinctual wishes and defensive needs (by fantasy). Such schemata serve the function of finding the object and structuring our knowledge of the external world. The functions of this type of identification are assigned to the reality ego. We have also observed that identifications can serve the function of the inner world and serve as substitutes for the loss of objects. There is a considerable body of psychoanalytic observation to support the generalization that in the process of mourning there is a heightened identification with the lost object. In subtle ways the individual assumes the characteristics of the loved person who has died. A similar process occurs in certain forms of depression, although in this case there is no actual loss of the object, but rather a loss of a love relationship with the object (Freud, 1917).

The term "identification" signifies the result of a synthetic and organizational function of the ego. Identification is a complex amalgam of the memories of perception and fantasies condensed and telescoped from many developmental phases. It is not a unitary, atomistic "thing in itself" (see criticism of representational psychology, Chapter V).

How do we then conceptualize this? Should we speak of separate identifications and conceptualize each change of function of an identification as a separate psychic structure? This would imply separate particles, or schemata, within the mind—shades of Locke's atomistic representational psychology. If neurophysiology were sufficiently advanced so that we knew that specific identifications could be correlated with specific reverberating circuits in the brain, the description of separate identifications as separate schemata might be justified. We do not, of course, possess any such knowledge (nor can we expect to). The concept of identification is purely psychological; it cannot rest upon any information gained from neurophysiology. We do not then feel entitled to describe separate structures when we are in fact describing separate *functions* of identification.

The model that we have introduced in Chapter VIII now enables us to clarify this problem. The superimposition of the topographic metaphor upon the structural makes it possible to describe change along two parameters, so that we are able to state that the same identification may serve different functions at different times. There is no need to postulate that with each change of function there is a change of structure.

Let us illustrate this principle by considering its application to the concept of the sense of identity. If we consider an identification to be the result of a historical process, an organized structure that is the product of time, the sense of identity is an analogous ego structure. But it is one that we can refer to metaphorically as "larger"—not simply the sum of identifications but a new synthesis. Now, the concept of self-representation was introduced by Hartmann (1950) in the following terms:

> It therefore would be clarifying if we define narcissism as the libidinal cathexis not of the ego but of the self. (It might also be useful to apply the term self-representation as opposed to object representation.) [p. 85].

Hartmann wished to make it clear that the *self* that Freud described as beloved in narcissistic states is not theoretically equivalent to the concept of the ego. Hartmann suggested that the self that is loved could be conceptualized as an ego structure—a *part* of the ego, but not equivalent to the concept of ego itself. In this sense the self representation is the antithesis of the object representation; the self may be loved in place of external objects. But we have also shown (in Chapter V) that the self representation is a structure that is essential to the process of the testing of reality. The development of a firm sense of identity is essential for the acceptance of the separateness of objects. Therefore, the structure of the self representation also serves an entirely different function. The self representation may be used as a substitute for an object in the sense that the term "narcissism" was originally used, or it may serve as a structure essential for the refinding of objects in the external world—a structure that underlies the capacity to accept the limitation of the loved objects and the limitation of reality. In one instance the functional system is allied to the inner world and in the other to the reality ego.

Should we, therefore, describe two self representations? As is true in the case of identification, it is simpler to conceptualize self representation as a structure whose function can alter according to whether gratification is sought from the inner world or from the environment. This functional alteration can be described as a topographic regression.

We can refer to separate ego structures—relatively persisting configurations that are the result of the ego's synthetic activity, which can serve different functional needs in accordance with the total situation of the organism at any given period of time.

In *The Unconscious,* Freud (1915b) considered the problem of whether conscious and unconscious ideas are recorded as separate registrations in the mind or whether the transposition between conscious and unconscious ideas represents a change of state:

When a psychical act (let us confine ourselves here to one which is in the nature of an idea) is transposed from the system *Ucs.* into the system *Cs.* (or *Pcs.*), are we to suppose that this transposition involves a fresh record—as it were, a second registration—of the idea in question, which may thus be situated as well in a fresh psychical locality, and alongside of which the original unconscious registration continues to exist? Or are we rather to believe that the transposition consists in a change in the state of the idea, a change involving the same material and occurring in the same locality? [p. 174].

He later answered this question by stating:

. . . the transition from the system *Ucs.* to the new system next to it is not effected through the making of a new registration but through a change in its state, an alteration in its cathexis [p. 180].

The concept that Freud was struggling with, that is, the concept of separate registrations, is similar to the problem that we have been outlining here—whether we should describe separate structures to represent functional changes. We have adapted Freud's answer. He preferred to use a topographic or functional metaphor, conceptualizing functional changes as changes in cathexis, rather than to postulate the existence of separate registrations or schemata.[1]

Primary Process and the Inner World

The relation of function to structure needs to be considered in another area, that is, in terms of primary and secondary process thinking. This designation does not refer to psychic structures (Beres, 1965) but is a consideration of form—it is a formal category of different modes of thinking. There is, however, a complication. Freud did not employ these terms to refer only to a formal designation but also

[1] Refer also to *The Interpretation of Dreams* (Freud, 1900, p. 610).

as an indication of fundamental distinction in the modes of functioning of the mental apparatus as a whole (Freud, 1940a). Freud described this fundamental distinction of different modes of mental functioning in terms of the metaphor of psychic energy.[2] Although Freud was clear that the concept of psychic energy had only a metaphoric relation to the energy of physical science, he retained a conviction that the distinction between *primary and secondary* process could be expressed as a distinction between *mobile and bound* energy.

What Freud designated as primary process thinking corresponds closely to Cassirer's designation of the mode of *mythical* thought. Although Freud's formulations antedate Cassirer's, Cassirer seems to have arrived at his conclusions independently. Primary process thinking is also referred to as "symbolic" thinking, although this designation is inaccurate, as secondary process thinking also uses a symbolic process. This issue will be discussed further. There remains, nevertheless, a rough equivalence between the concepts of primary process, symbolic thinking, and mythical thought.

Freud's most complete description of the primary and secondary process can be found in *The Interpretation of Dreams* (Freud, 1900). His enumeration of the qualities of the primary process follows:

> (1) The intensities of the individual ideas . . . pass over from one idea to the other. . . . Here we have the fact of 'compression' or 'condensation,' which has become familiar in the dream work. (2) Owing once more to the freedom with which the intensities can be transferred, 'intermediate ideas' resembling compromises are constructed under the sway of condensation. (3) The ideas which transfer their intensities to each

2 The wish to formulate laws of mental functioning in terms of energy transformations has been traced to the influence upon Freud of the school of Helmholtz (Bernfeld, 1944), who was dedicated to the belief that biological and psychological phenomena could be fully described by means of physical laws.

other stand in the loosest mutual relations. They are linked by associations of a kind that is scorned by our normal thinking and relegated to the use of jokes. (4) Thoughts which are mutually contradictory make no attempt to do away with each other, but persist side by side. . . . It will be seen that the chief characteristic of these processes is that the whole stress is laid upon making the cathecting energy mobile and capable of discharge [p. 595].

In the same work, Freud also states that the primary process is "unable to do anything but wish." It is a system seeking immediate discharge and a "perceptual identity" with the object, with the memory of the experience of satisfaction.

The secondary process, however, has abandoned this intention and taken another in its place—the establishment of a *'thought* identity' (with that experience). All thinking is no more than a circuitous path from the memory of a satisfaction (a memory which has been adapted as a purposive idea) to an identical cathexis of the same memory which it is hoped to attain once more through an intermediate stage of motor experiences [p. 602].

The secondary system utilizes smaller quantities of bound energy. It functions in accord with the reality principle and "by interposing the processes of thinking, it secures a postponement of motor discharges and controls the access to motility" (Freud, 1923, p. 55).

Thought was considered by Freud (1911a) to be a trial action. The secondary process is conceived of as inhibitory, in contrast to the primary process which seeks discharge and satisfaction.

Cassirer's concept of mythical thought shows, as we have said, a striking similarity to Freud's concept of the primary process. Both men considered a designation of thought which appeared earlier in man's history than did logical or scientific thought. It is a form of thought that is more primitive, yet it persists after man's acquisition of logical modes of thinking. For Cassirer, mythical thought is a mode that makes no sharp distinctions between inner and outer, between subject and object. Symbols are *not* used in a denotive sense; they possess a sensory immediacy and cannot be separated from the objects in the external world that they represent. The symbol and the object are one. Cassirer attributed to this mode of thought a sense of timelessness reminiscent of Freud's description of the unconscious. Cassirer stated further that the form and function of this entire mode is dominated by "omnipotence of thought and omnipotence of desire." For Cassirer, as for Freud, the secondary mode of thinking entails a form of delay or distancing; there is not the sensory immediacy of the mythical or magical mode. Freud and Cassirer both considered the secondary system to be a later phylogenetic and ontogenetic acquisition. Cassirer indicated that at a certain point in development the child learns "the representative function of names" which changes his entire relation to reality. The symbol is then used in its denotive function, whereas in the mythical mode of thought the symbol and the object symbolized are inseparable.

The concepts of the inner world, of the Janus-faced organization of the ego, and of the concept of topographic regression all can be subsumed under the formalism of the primary process. When we describe the inner world as an alternative source of gratification, we have not added anything to Freud's description of the primary process whose fundamental characteristic was gratification by means of the wish.

The inner world provides for the metaphoric or symbolic representation of the relationships between the individual and the external world. Under the domination of the omnipotent wish there is a plastic transformation of these events. You will recall Freud's example of the infant who, in his mother's absence, drops and retrieves a spool on a string over the edge of his crib. The event "in reality," the separation from mother, is symbolically re-created with the roles of the actors interchanged—the helpless child now controls the mother. I would suggest that this example in its simplicity is paradigmatic of the primary process's capacity for plastic transformation in accordance with need.

Throughout this work we have stressed that there is a twofold relation to the environment—one in accordance with the inner world or primary process, the other in accordance with the reality ego, which apprehends that which corresponds to events in the external world. The inner world has its origin in an animistic world view, a world view dominated by man's helplessness in the face of separation and death. The reality ego, while ontogenetically of later origin, has vestigial representation in infancy (Hartmann, 1956). That is to say, the ego in its preadaptive potentiality possesses the capacity to structure perceptual processes as is necessary for survival. This preadaptive "fitting in to the environment" has phylogenetic parallels in earlier forms of animal life that also correspond to the concept of the "umwelt" of Von Uexküll (1934). I have interpreted the capacity to differentiate the self from the object as described by Piaget and Spitz as illustrative of the unfolding of this early autonomous reality ego, the mode of functioning which corresponds to the formalism of the secondary process.

Two Forms of Symbolic Function: Private and Public

Knowledge of the environment is vouchsafed by the earliest stages of the preadaptive ego (the primary autonomy of Hartmann)—a vestige of our evolutionary inheritance. With the development of the capacity to form the first object relationship, knowledge of the environment will also be acquired culturally. Culture in man then will assume the task that is assumed by instinct in lower animals. Knowledge of this sort is acquired through the medium of language. Language is, of course, a symbolic process, but the symbolic function here differs from that attributed to the primary process. In this instance, the function is such as to ensure a correspondence between the object symbolized and the symbol. Secondary process thinking is directed toward action upon the environment. It acknowledges "things as they are" and hence accepts the need for delay. Secondary process thinking is *object-directed*—it is *social*. Primary process thinking is *personal*—it is dominated by the omnipotent wish. The communicative aspects of secondary process thinking involve the acquisition of rules for communication. The study of modern linguistics has suggested that there is a strict lawfulness of communicated speech (Chomsky, 1965). Wittgenstein (1958) proposed that meaning is derived from rules, that learning language is akin to learning a game with specified rules. Secondary-process thinking entails the adaptation of culturally conventionalized modes as opposed to the private creativity of primary-process thinking (Kubie, 1953).

As we noted earlier, the term "symbolic process" has been traditionally a reference to the primary process. But as we have just indicated, secondary processes must also involve some form of symbolic thought. This problem has been noted by Rycroft (1956) and Beres (1960). Rycroft suggests (as does Kubie) that "symbolism is a general capacity which may be used in different ways." On the other hand, Beres preferred to speak of two forms of symbolism. Whether we give a name to a change of function is, I believe, a semantic issue. There are two different forms of symbolic process corresponding to the private and public functions of the primary and secondary processes.[3]

---

[3] It is important to note that the use of the word "symbol" is different from that ordinarily employed in psychoanalytic writing. Jones (1916), for example, in his classic paper on symbolism, would restrict the term "symbol" to only that which denotes something that requires repression. So that symbolism in psychoanalytic terminology, as we indicated, has usually referred to primary process symbolism.

Cassirer has further clarified this problem by establishing a distinction between the symbol that denotes the object and the symbol that *is* the object. However, as we emphasized, we believe the essential distinction is the function for which the symbolism is employed; the metaphorical symbolism of the primary process is essentially private, whereas the symbolism of the secondary process is object-related, conventionalized, and subject to linguistically determined rules.

We have not presented here anything that is essentially new or in contradiction of Freud's basic concept of the primary and secondary process. However, I would suggest that our more recent knowledge, gained from the treatment of borderline and schizophrenic patients, compels us to reconsider Freud's belief that the *fundamental* distinction between the primary and secondary process is energic. This may be one-sided and restricting and has led, in modern psychoanalytic theorizing, to highly abstract distinctions regarding the state of instinctual energy.

The energic metaphor may obscure what may be more compelling functional considerations—whether gratification is sought from the inner world or from external objects.

It was noted early in the history of psychoanalysis that the symbols employed in dreams (private symbols) may be used to denote the same objects as do the symbols that are public, such as the symbols of mythology and religion (Jones, 1916). This observation became the central thesis of Jung's psychology; he denied that symbols were created anew in individual development but instead thought that they were actually inherited as the "collective unconscious." Such a belief rests on the uncritical acceptance of Lamarck's doctrine of the inheritance of acquired characteristics, for which there is no scientific evidence.

Yet there is truth to the observation that the symbols employed by the primary process may in *some* instances not be idiosyncratic creations but are shared. One does not have to invoke the concept of a collective inheritance of racial memories in order to explain this observation. There are alternative possibilities. There is a certain universality to the content of that which is symbolized—interest in genitals, concern about the mystery of birth, fear of death, etc., are basic concerns, common to all people. The similarity between elongated objects and the phallus is sufficiently obvious so that this type of symbolization needs no inherited knowledge. In ancient Sumerian mythology, emergence from the water is the customary symbol for creativity and birth (Frankfort, et al., 1949). Psychoanalytic patients who have no knowledge of ancient mythology also may employ water to represent birth in dreams. The origin of the choice of symbol may be nothing more than the common recognition that water has a creative power—when the earth is watered it produces life. Let us consider a third example of commonly held symbolism. In psychoanalytic practice, many psychoanalysts have observed that the spider is used to symbolize a conception of the mother that is formed perhaps during the second year of life. It is an early image. At these times the spider is used to symbolize not the mother as a whole but more specifically her genital area. The near universality of this symbol again appears to be a puzzle. But its origin may be traced to something that most children have experienced—that is, a view, however fleeting, of the mother's genital area. To the child this would appear as something dark in the middle surrounded by grasping appendages, the thighs. The spider is thus ready made to symbolize and maintain under repression this early perception.

Symbolism to be effective cannot be a cliché. The far-reaching influence of Freud's discoveries has restricted the availability for use of the more obvious symbols. Today's sophisticated dreamer cannot as easily as her Victorian counterpart disguise her thoughts concerning the penis by dreaming of snakes. The view that each person constructs his own symbolic equation is, however, an oversimplification. The relation between private and public symbolism is more complex. The culture may perpetuate ancient symbolic equations, which may be unconsciously assimilated; the symbolic forms may be perpetuated by culture without invoking genetic inheritance as an explanation. I quote from Jones (1916):

> Symbolism thus appears as the unconscious precipitate of primitive means of adaptation to reality that have become superfluous and useless, a sort of lumber room of civilization to which the adult readily flees in states of reduced or deficient capacity for adaptation to reality, in order to regain his old, long-forgotten playthings of childhood. What later generations know and regard only as a symbol had in earlier stages of mental life full and real meaning and value [p. 109].

The symbolic function of paleolithic art described in Chapter II provides an example of Jones's concept of symbolism as an earlier mode of adaptation to reality. Although there is much that we do not know of this ancient Stone Age religion, whose cave paintings served as ritualized images, we can be reasonably certain that the paintings served to assure the cycle of creation and killing of animals, a cycle necessary for the sustenance of life. The symbolism may, as recent authorities suggest, refer to a more extended metaphysical world view; the visual ritual may also control human creation and death (Leroi-Gourham, 1966). Regardless of whatever is finally learned concerning the specific interpretation of the cave paintings, we can be assured that they were vital to paleolithic man's adaptation to his environment.

The history of religion shares with man's unconscious mind a fundamental conservatism—anything that has once been of value survives although it may be altered and bear no direct resemblance to the original structure. G. Rachel Levy (1963)

has demonstrated that this paleolithic Stone Age religion
has survived as significant elements of Western religious
thought. Earlier symbolic representations are preserved by
culture; symbolism need not be completely discovered anew
by each individual—he may assimilate through visual or
other means symbolic forms that are remnants of an archaic
past.

Paleolithic art is creative in a literal sense. The symbolic
form gives life, it literally *creates* the object. Although the
origin of this art is unknown, it too must have had its cre-
ator. That is, creation, whether of art or of science, has its
origin as a private vision. The free range of the primary
process permits a new combination of elements. "The symbol and the metaphor are as necessary to science as to poetry"
(Bronowski, 1956). Creativity takes place in the primary
process as a private function and is then communicated and
given conventionalized form by the secondary process. It is
then shared and made public; *private and public modes of
thinking interpenetrate.* This idea was originally proposed
by Cassirer (1953) and has been expressed in varying forms
as a basic description of the creative process by Kris (1950),
Milner (1955), Winnicott (1951), Rycroft (1956), and others.

Culture originates in the private vision of the primary
process. This vision is externalized and given conventionalized structure through the process of group identification,
a form of object relation (as we have described in Chapter
VI).

The original creative process and the elaborative secondary
process cannot be separated from the theory of object relations. The primary process, based on the omnipotence of the
wish, transforms symbols plastically in accordance with instinctive and defensive needs. We have stressed the fundamental need—to minimize the danger of separation and loss.
The creative process, as Milner suggests, is a creative illusion that contains, as does the development of transference in

psychoanalytic treatment, an element of illusory connectedness between the subject and object.

The secondary process which entails an acknowledgment
of "otherness," an acceptance of the conventionalized rules
of communication, embodies an acceptance of the limitation
of the self. There is acceptance of the need of others to com-
prehend. In the acknowledgment of the needs of others there
is implicit an awareness of the fact that others exist as
separate from the self—a limitation of narcissism.[4] There is
a unity between the creation of a cultural form and the creation of the image of a loved object. Both involve the interpenetration of the private vision with the public, conventionalized schemata; that is, the modes of loving and knowing
are inseparable.

---

4 We do not wish to imply that those people who cannot accept the separateness of objects are incapable of using secondary process thinking. We have
throughout suggested that certain autonomous functions of the reality ego are
retained, and to this extent there are certain areas of mature ego functioning
even in those people who are considered psychotic. This observation has been
formulated by Freud as a split in the ego, an acknowledgment that more
mature modes of ego functioning can exist side by side with more archaic ones.

REFERENCES

Abraham, K. (1924), A Short Study of the Development of the Libido, Viewed in the Light of Mental Disorders. *Selected Papers on Psychoanalysis.* London: Hogarth Press, 1948, pp. 418–501.

Arlow, J. and Brenner, C. (1964), *Psychoanalytic Concepts and Structural Theory.* New York: International Universities Press.

Barrett, W. (1962), Phenomenology and Existentialism. *Philosophy in the Twentieth Century,* eds. W. Barrett and H. Aiken. New York: Random House, pp. 125–169.

Bataille, G. (1955), *Lascaux or the Birth of Art.* Cleveland: World Publishing.

Benedek, T. (1949), The Psychosomatic Implications of the Primary Unit: Mother-Child. *Amer. J. Orthopsychiat.,* 19: 642–654.

Beres, D. (1965), Structure and Function in Psychoanalysis. *Internat. J. Psychoanal.,* 46: 53–63.

—— (1960), Perception, Imagination and Reality. *Internat. J. Psychoanal.,* 41: 327–334.

Berlin, I. (1956), Locke. In *The Age of Enlightenment.* New York: Mentor, pp. 30–112.

Bernfeld, S. (1944), Freud's Earliest Theories and the School of Helmholtz. *Psychoanal. Quart.,* 13: 341–362.

Bion, W. R. (1959), Attacks on Linking. *Internat. J. Psychoanal.,* 40: 308–315.

Bowlby, J. (1960), Separation Anxiety. *Internat. J. Psychoanal.,* 41: 89–113.

Brain, W. R. (1951), *Mind, Perception and Science*. Oxford: Blackwell.

Breuil, H. and Obermaier, H. (1935), *The Cave of Altimara*. Madrid: Tipografia De Archivos.

Broadbent, D. E. (1965), Information Processing in the Nervous System. *Science*, 150: 457–462.

Bronowski, J. (1956), *Science and Human Values*. New York: Harper Torchbook, 1959.

Buber, M. (1958), *I and Thou*. New York: Scribner's.

Cassirer, E. (1953), *The Philosophy of Symbolic Forms*. New Haven: Yale University Press.

Childe, V. G. (1951), *Man Makes Himself*. New York: Mentor Books.

Chomsky, N. (1965), *Aspects of the Theory of Syntax*. Cambridge: M.I.T. Press.

Deutsch, H. (1942), Some Forms of Emotional Disturbances and Their Relationship to Schizophrenia. *Neuroses and Character Types*. New York: International Universities Press, 1965, pp. 262–281.

Eddington, A. (1928), *The Nature of the Physical World*. Ann Arbor: University of Michigan Press, 1958.

Erikson, E. (1959), Identity and the Life Cycle. *Psychological Issues*, Monograph 1. New York: International Universities Press.

—— (1965), Psychoanalysis and Ongoing History: Problems of Identity, Hatred and Nonviolence. *Amer. J. Psychiat.*, 122: 241–250.

Fairbairn, W. R. D. (1940), Schizoid Factors in the Personality. In *Object-Relations Theory of Personality*. New York: Basic Books, 1954, pp. 3–27.

—— (1952), *Psychoanalytic Studies of the Personality*. London: Tavistock.

—— (1963), Synopsis of an Object Relations Theory of the Personality. *Internat. J. Psychoanal.*, 44: 224–225.

Federn, P. (1952), *Ego Psychology and the Psychoses*. New York: Basic Books.

Fenichel, O. (1926), Identification. In *The Collected Papers of Otto Fenichel*, 1: 97–112. New York: W. W. Norton, 1953.

168 *References*

Ferenczi, S. (1913), Stages in the Development of the Sense of
Reality. *Sex in Psychoanalysis.* New York: Brunner, 1950.

Frankfort, H., Frankfort, H. A., Wilson, J. A., and Jacobsen, T.
(1949), *Before Philosophy.* Baltimore: Penguin Books.

Frazer, T. G. (1890), *The New Golden Bough.* New York: Cri-
terion Books, 1959.

Freud, A. (1936), *The Ego and the Mechanisms of Defense* (Re-
vised Edition). New York: International Universities Press,
1967.

——— (1951), Observations on Child Development. *The Psychoanalytic Study of the Child,* 6: 18–30. New York: International
Universities Press.

——— (1952), The Mutual Influences in the Development of
Ego and Id. *The Psychoanalytic Study of the Child,* 7: 42–50.
New York: International Universities Press.

——— and Burlingham, D. (1944), *War and Children.* New York:
International Universities Press.

———, Schur, M., and Spitz, R. (1960), Discussion of paper
"Grief and Mourning in Infancy," by Bowlby, J. *The Psycho-
analytic Study of the Child,* 15: 53–94. New York: International
Universities Press.

Freud, S. (1891), *On Aphasia.* New York: International Universities Press, 1953.

——— and Breuer, J. (1895), Studies on Hysteria. *Standard Edition,* 2. London: Hogarth Press, 1955.

——— (1900), The Interpretation of Dreams. *Standard Edition,*
4 & 5. London: Hogarth Press, 1953.

——— (1911a), Formulations on the Two Principles of Mental
Functioning. *Standard Edition,* 12: 218–226. London: Hogarth
Press, 1957.

——— (1911b), Psychoanalytic Notes on an Autobiographical Account of a Case of Paranoia (Dementia Paranoides). *Standard
Edition,* 12: 3–80. London: Hogarth Press, 1958.

——— (1912), The Dynamics of Transference. *Standard Edition,*
12: 99–108. London: Hogarth Press, 1958.

——— (1913), Totem and Taboo. *Standard Edition,* 13: 1–161.
London: Hogarth Press, 1955.

———— (1914), On Narcissism: An Introduction. *Standard Edition,* 14: 67–102. London: Hogarth Press, 1957.

———— (1915a), Instincts and their Vicissitudes. *Standard Edition,* 14: 109–140. London: Hogarth Press, 1957.

———— (1915b), The Unconscious. *Standard Edition,* 14: 159–215. London: Hogarth Press, 1957.

———— (1917), Mourning and Melancholia. *Standard Edition,* 14: 237–258. London: Hogarth Press, 1957.

———— (1920), Beyond the Pleasure Principle. *Standard Edition,* 18: 3–64. London: Hogarth Press, 1955.

———— (1921), Group Psychology and the Analysis of the Ego. *Standard Edition,* 18: 67–143. London: Hogarth Press, 1955.

———— (1923), The Ego and the Id. *Standard Edition,* 19: 3–66. London: Hogarth Press, 1957.

———— (1924a), The Loss of Reality in Neurosis and Psychosis. *Standard Edition,* 19: 183–187. London: Hogarth Press, 1957.

———— (1924b), The Economic Problem of Masochism. *Standard Edition,* 19: 157–170. London: Hogarth Press, 1957.

———— (1925), Negation. *Standard Edition,* 19: 235–239. London: Hogarth Press, 1957.

———— (1926), Inhibitions, Symptoms and Anxiety. *Standard Edition,* 20: 77–174. London: Hogarth Press, 1959.

———— (1927), Fetishism. *Standard Edition,* 21: 149–157. London: Hogarth Press, 1961.

———— (1930), Civilization and Its Discontents. *Standard Edition,* 21: 59–145. London: Hogarth Press, 1961.

———— (1940a), An Outline of Psychoanalysis. *Standard Edition,* 23: 141–207. London: Hogarth Press, 1964.

———— (1940b), Splitting of the Ego in the Process of Defence. *Standard Edition,* 23: 271–278. London: Hogarth Press, 1964.

Frosch, J. (1964), The Psychotic Character: Clinical and Psychiatric Considerations. *Psychiat. Quart.,* 38: 81–96.

Gill, M. M. and Brenman, M. (1959), *Hypnosis and Related States.* New York: International Universities Press.

Gill, M. M. (1963), Topography and Systems in Psychoanalytic Theory. In *Psychological Issues.* New York: International Universities Press.

Gitelson, M. (1958), On Ego Distortion. *Internat. J. Psychoanal.*, 29: 245–257.

Glover, E. (1956), *On the Early Development of the Mind.* New York: International Universities Press.

———— (1966), Metapsychology or Metaphysics. A Psychoanalytic Essay. *Psychoanal. Quart.*, 35: 173–190.

Gombrich, E. H. (1960), *Art and Illusion.* New York: Pantheon.

Graziosi, P. (1960), *Palaeolithic Art.* London: Faber and Faber.

Greenacre, P. (1958), Early Physical Determinants in the Development of the Sense of Identity. *J. Amer. Psychoanal. Assn.*, 6: 612–627.

Greene, T. M. (1929), *Introduction to Kant Selections.* New York: Charles Scribner's Sons.

Greenson, R. (1953), The Struggle Against Identification. *J. Amer. Psychoanal. Assn.*, 1: 538–539.

Hartmann, H. (1939), *Ego Psychology and the Problem of Adaptation.* New York: International Universities Press, 1958.

———— (1950), Comments on the Psychoanalytic Theory of the Ego. *The Psychoanalytic Study of the Child,* 5: 74–96. New York: International Universities Press.

———— (1953), Contributions to the Metapsychology of Schizophrenia. *The Psychoanalytic Study of the Child,* 8: 177–198. New York: International Universities Press.

———— (1956), Notes on the Reality Principle. *The Psychoanalytic Study of the Child,* 11: 31–53. New York: International Universities Press.

Hendrick, I. (1936), Ego Development and Certain Character Problems. *Psychoanal. Quart.*, 5: 320–346.

———— (1951), Early Development of the Ego: Identification in Infancy. *Psychoanal. Quart.*, 20: 44–61.

Hoffer, W. (1949), Mouth, Hand and Ego Integration. *The Psychoanalytic Study of the Child,* 3/4: 49–56. New York: International Universities Press.

Home, H. J. (1966), The Concept of Mind. *Internat. J. Psychoanal.*, 47: 43–49.

Hume, D. (1739–1740), *Treatise on Human Nature.* New York: Dolphin Book, Doubleday & Co., 1961.

Jacobson, E. (1954), Contribution to the Metapsychology of Psychotic Identifications. *J. Amer. Psychoanal. Assn.,* 2: 239–262.
———— (1964), *The Self and the Object World.* New York: International Universities Press.
James, W. (1890), *The Principles of Psychology,* Vol. II. New York: Dover, 1950.
———— (1902), *The Varieties of Religious Experience.* New York: Mentor Books, 1958.
Jones, E. (1913), The God Complex. *Essays in Applied Psycho-Analysis.* New York: International Universities Press, 1964, pp. 244–265.
———— (1916), The Theory of Symbolism. *Papers in Psycho-Analysis.* London: Bailliere, Tindall and Cox, 1948.
Keynes, J. M. (1956), *Essays and Sketches in Biography.* New York: Meridian.
Klein, M. (1940), Mourning and Its Relation to Manic-Depressive States. *Contributions to Psycho-Analysis.* London: Hogarth Press, 1948, pp. 311–388.
———— (1946), Notes on Some Schizoid Mechanisms. *Internat. J. Psychoanal.,* 27: 99–110.
Knight, R. (1954), Borderline States. *Psychoanalytic Psychiatry and Psychology.* New York: International Universities Press.
Koestler, A. (1964), *The Act of Creation.* London: Hutchinson.
Kris, E. (1935), The Psychology of Caricature. *Psychoanalytic Explorations in Art.* New York: International Universities Press, 1952, pp. 173–188.
———— (1950), On Preconscious Mental Processes. *Psychoanalytic Explorations in Art.* New York: International Universities Press, 1952, pp. 303–320.
Kubie, L. S. (1953), The Distortion of the Symbolic Process in Neurosis and Psychosis. *J. Amer. Psychoanal. Assn.,* 1: 59–86.
Kuhn, T. S. (1962), *The Structure of Scientific Revolutions.* Chicago: The University of Chicago Press.
Laming, A. (1959), *Lascaux.* Baltimore: Penguin Books.
Leroi-Gourham, A. (1966), *Treasures of Prehistoric Art.* New York: Harry N. Abrams.
Levi-Strauss, C. (1963), *Totemism.* Boston: Beacon Press.

Levy, G. R. (1963), *Religious Conceptions of the Stone Age.* New York: Harper and Row.

Lewin, B. D. (1928), *Dreams and the Uses of Regression.* New York: International Universities Press, 1958.

———— (1950), *The Psychoanalysis of Elation.* New York: Mentor.

Lichtenstein, H. (1961) , Identity and Sexuality: A Study of Their Interrelationship in Man. *J. Amer. Psychoanal. Assn.,* 9:179–260.

Loewald, H. (1951), Ego and Reality. *Internat. J. Psychoanal.,* 32: 10–18.

———— (1960), On the Therapeutic Action of Psychoanalysis. *Internat. J. Psychoanal.,* 41: 16–33.

Lorenz, K. (1954), *Man Meets Dog.* London: Methuen.

———— (1963), *On Aggression.* New York: Harcourt, Brace and World.

———— (1965), *Evolution and Modifications of Behavior.* Chicago: The University of Chicago Press.

Macalpine, I. and Hunter, R. (1955), *Daniel Paul Schreber, Memoirs of My Nervous Illness.* London: Dawson.

Mahler, M. (1963), Thoughts about Development and Individuation. *The Psychoanalytic Study of the Child,* 18: 307–324. New York: International Universities Press.

Mayr, E. (1963), *Animal Species and Evolution.* Cambridge: Harvard University Press.

Menninger, K., Moynan, M., and Pruyser, P. (1963), *The Vital Balance.* New York: Viking.

Milner, M. (1955), The Role of Illusion in Symbol Formation. In *New Directions in Psychoanalysis,* eds. M. Klein, M. Heiman, and R. E. Money-Kyrle. New York: Basic Books, pp. 82–108.

Modell, A. H. (1958), The Theoretical Implication of Hallucinatory Experiences in Schizophrenia. *J. Amer. Psychoanal. Assn.,* 6: 442–480.

———— (1960), An Approach to the Nature of Auditory Hallucinations in Schizophrenia. *Arch. Gen. Psychiat.,* 3: 259–266.

———— (1961), Denial and the Sense of Separateness. *J. Amer. Psychoanal. Assn.,* 9: 533–547.

———— (1963), Primitive Object Relationships and the Predisposition to Schizophrenia. *Internat. J. Psychoanal.,* 44: 282–292.

——— (1965), On Having the Right to a Life. *Internat. J. Psychoanal.,* 46: 323–331.

Murray, G. (1951), *Five Stages of Greek Religion.* New York: Doubleday.

Nunberg, H. (1951), Transference and Reality. In *Practice and Theory of Psychoanalysis,* Vol. II. New York: International Universities Press, 1965, pp. 118–133.

Piaget, J. (1954), *The Construction of Reality in the Child.* New York: Basic Books.

Portmann, A. (1961), *Animals as Social Beings.* New York: Harper & Row.

Provence, S. and Ritvo, S. (1961), Effects of Deprivation on Institutionalized Infants: Disturbances in Development of Relationship to Inanimate Objects. *The Psychoanalytic Study of the Child,* 16: 189–205. New York: International Universities Press.

Provence, S. and Lipton, R. (1962), *Infants in Institutions.* New York: International Universities Press.

Read, H. (1965), *Icon and Idea.* New York: Schocken.

Ritvo, S. and Solnit, A. J. (1958), Influences of Early Mother-Child Interactions on Identification Process. *The Psychoanalytic Study of the Child,* 13: 64–85. New York: International Universities Press.

Rochlin, G. (1965), *Griefs and Discontents.* Boston: Little Brown.

Roffwarg, H. P., Muzio, J. W., and Dement, W. C. (1966), Ontogenic Development of the Human Sleep-Dream Cycle. *Science,* 152: 235–258.

Róheim, G. (1955), *Magic and Schizophrenia.* New York: International Universities Press.

Russell, B. (1948), *Human Knowledge.* New York: Simon and Schuster.

Rycroft, C. (1955), Two Notes on Idealization, Illusion and Disillusion as Normal and Abnormal Psychological Processes. *Internat. J. Psychoanal.,* 36: 81–87.

——— (1956), Symbolism and Its Relationship to the Primary and Secondary Processes. *Internat. J. Psychoanal.,* 37: 137–146.

Ryle, G. (1949), *The Concept of Mind.* New York: Barnes and Noble, 1965.

Sandler, J. and Rosenblatt, B. (1962), The Concept of the Representational World. *The Psychoanalytic Study of the Child,* 17: 128–145. New York: International Universities Press.

Searles, H. (1960), *The Nonhuman Environment.* New York: International Universities Press.

—— (1965), *Collected Papers on Schizophrenia and Related Subjects.* New York: International Universities Press.

Singer, C., Holmyard, E. J., and Hall, A. R. (1954), *A History of Technology,* Vol. I. London: Oxford University Press.

Singer, I. (1966), *The Nature of Love: Plato to Luther.* New York: Random House.

Slocum, J. (1890), *Sailing Alone Around the World.* New York: Dover, 1956.

Snyder, F. (1966), Toward an Evolutionary Theory of Dreaming. *Amer. J. Psychiat.,* 123: 121–142.

Spitz, R. (1945), Hospitalism. *The Psychoanalytic Study of the Child,* 1: 53–74. New York: International Universities Press.

—— (1965), *The First Year of Life.* New York: International Universities Press.

Stone, L. (1954), The Widening Scope of Indications for Psychoanalysis. *J. Amer. Psychoanal. Assn.,* 2: 567–594.

—— (1961), *The Psychoanalytic Situation.* New York: International Universities Press.

Storch, A. (1924), *The Primitive Forms of Inner Experiences and Thought in Schizophrenia.* New York: Nervous and Mental Diseases Publishing Co.

Sullivan, H. S. (1953), *The Interpersonal Theory of Psychiatry.* New York: Norton.

Tidd, C. W., Bowlby, J., and Kaufman, C. (1960), Symposium on Psycho-Analysis and Ethology. *Internat. J. Psychoanal.,* 41: 308–312.

Von Bertalanffy, L. (1964), The Mind-Body Problem: A New View. *Psychosom. Med.,* 26: 29–45.

Von Uexküll, J. (1934), A Stroll through the Worlds of Animals and Men. In *Instinctive Behavior,* ed. C. Schiller. New York: International Universities Press, 1957, pp. 5–80.

Von Weizsacker, C. F. (1964), *The Relevance of Science*. New York: Harper and Row.

Waelder, R. (1960), *Basic Theory of Psychoanalysis*. New York: International Universities Press.

Weber, M. (1922), *The Sociology of Religion*. Boston: Beacon Press, 1963.

Weisman, A. (1965), *The Existential Core of Psychoanalysis*. Boston: Little Brown.

Whorf, B. L. (1956), *Language, Thought and Reality*. Cambridge: M.I.T. Press, 1964.

Wigner, E. P. (1964), Events, Laws of Nature and Invariance Problems. *Science,* 145: 995–999.

Winnicott, D. W. (1945), Primitive Emotional Development. In *Collected Papers*. New York: Basic Books, 1958.

—— (1951), Transitional Objects and Transitional Phenomena. In *Collected Papers*. New York: Basic Books, 1958, pp. 229–242.

—— (1960), Ego Distortion in Terms of True and False Self. *The Maturational Processes and the Facilitating Environment*. New York: International Universities Press, 1965, pp. 140–152.

—— (1962), Ego Integration in Child Development. *The Maturational Processes and the Facilitating Environment*. New York: International Universities Press, 1965, pp. 56–63.

Wittgenstein, L. (1958), *The Blue and Brown Books*. New York: Harper Torchbook, 1965.

Zetzel, E. (1956a), Current Concepts of Transference. *Internat. J. Psychoanal.,* 37: 369–376.

—— (1956b), An Approach to the Relation between Concept and Content in Psychoanalytic Theory. *The Psychoanalytic Study of the Child,* 11:99–121. New York: International Universities Press.

—— (1965a), The Theory of Therapy in Relation to a Developmental Model of the Psychic Apparatus. *Internat. J. Psychoanal.,* 46: 39–52.

—— (1965b), Depression and the Incapacity to Bear It. *Drives, Affects and Behavior,* Vol. II, ed. M. Schur. New York: International Universities Press, pp. 243–274.

Zeuner, F. E. (1954), Domestication of Animals. *A History of Technology,* Vol. I., ed. C. Singer et al. London: Oxford University Press, pp. 327–352.

Zimmer, H. (1951), *Philosophies of India.* Cleveland: World Publishing, 1964.

INDEX